LEADERSHIP IN CRISIS

KENNIKAT PRESS

NATIONAL UNIVERSITY PUBLICATIONS

SERIES IN AMERICAN STUDIES

General Editor

JAMES P. SHENTON

Professor of History, Columbia University

Gloria J. Barron

LEADERSHIP

IN

CRISIS

FDR AND THE PATH TO INTERVENTION

National University Publications
KENNIKAT PRESS ● 1973
Port Washington, N.Y. · London

Library of Congress Catalog Card No: 73–75576
ISBN: 0–8046–9038–3

Manufactured in the United States of America

Published by
Kennikat Press, Inc.
Port Washington, N.Y./London

ACKNOWLEDGMENTS

It gives me much pleasure to acknowledge the many people to whom I have become indebted in the course of researching and writing this book. The American Association of University Women assisted me with the Meta Glass Fellowship in 1968-1969, making possible an initially uninterrupted period of time for research and writing. I am grateful to Dr. Elizabth B. Drewry, former Director of the Franklin D. Roosevelt Library, Mr. Joseph W. Marshall, Librarian, and their fine staff for their helpful and always courteous assistance. I also wish to thank Dr. Paul T. Heffron of the Library of Congress Manuscript Division and Mr. John E. Taylor of the National Archives for their interest and help. I appreciate, too, the time taken by Dr. S. Everett Gleason, of the State Department's Historical Office and the coauthor of the Langer and Gleason books, to talk with me informally about the subject. Professor William Yandell Elliott, of Harvard University and American University, offered invaluable advice and assistance at the early stages of the work, for which I am most appreciative.

I am so very grateful to the following people I have interviewed for a very generous amount of time and for the courtesy and patience with which they responded to my questions: Joseph W. Alsop, Andrew Berding, Adolf A. Berle, Raymond P. Brandt, Benjamin V. Cohen, Thomas G. Corcoran, Ernest Cuneo, Anna Roosevelt Halsted (Mrs. James A.), Arthur Krock, Claude Pepper, Samuel I. Rosenman, and Benjamin Welles.

For their encouragement and advice at many stages of the research and writing I am especially indebted to Professors Aubrey L. Parkman and Russell E. Miller of Tufts University. Professor Parkman, who supervised it as a doctoral dissertation, has taken a constructive and indefatigable interest in this work and has helped to improve its structure while at the same time allowing that necessary freedom that made the writing an enjoyable experience. More than I can acknowledge in words I owe him a very special debt.

For the typing of the manuscript I was fortunate to have the excellent assistance of Miss Dorothy Littlefield.

Finally, I wish to thank my father and pay tribute to the memory of my mother. It was their special encouragement that made this work possible, and to them it is devotedly dedicated.

PREFACE

In the thirties, a time when the western European democracies were afflicted with both weak, irresolute leadership and an inordinate fear of communism, Franklin Roosevelt was far in advance of most statesmen of the world in coming to an early appreciation of the Nazi menace. Yet as a democratic leader, but one with weak allies in Europe, and at the same time the leader of a country seriously and perilously beset with its own domestic problems, he could hardly be said to have had free will in the fashioning of United States foreign policy. Perhaps no democratic leader, responsible always at the bar of public opinion, does. It is the purpose of this story of Roosevelt's struggle with foreign policy in the thirties, and more particularly in the years immediately preceding America's entry into World War II, to probe the ambivalence and ambiguities of democratic leadership. The purpose is also to study the reactions of a man totally dedicated and peculiarly able, a man possessed of a rare understanding of what leadership is all about, to the inexorable forces of chance and necessity.

Franklin Roosevelt prided himself on being a "realist" and most of all a politician. The first imperative, as he saw it, was to get elected. Next, it was vital to avoid a substantial loss of popular support, which would not only threaten his programs but imperil the viability of his administration. The goal was to gain and keep as much public backing as possible for the course he felt necessary th chart for the general well-being of the country. This was no easy matter in the thirties, an age of fears, hatreds, intolerances, and very little absorption as yet of twentieth-century immigrant stock, with its varying religious and ethnic composition, into the mainstream of American life.

Roosevelt's technique, astutely surmised by George VI, King of England, was, in the King's own words, to "[lead] public opinion by allowing it to get ahead of you." After the outbreak of World War II in Europe, as he took steps to sustain Allied, in particular British, morale and their war effort, Roosevelt did so only after appearing to lag behind public opinion and to have been goaded into action by an impatient citizenry. Once in a while he himself would even provide the spur, by hinting to specific representatives of interventionist groups that goading was currently in order.

At times he publicly maintained that the steps toward involvement, Lend-Lease for instance, were efforts toward peace rather than war, while all the while realizing full well, by mid-1940, that the entrance of the United States into World War II was inevitable. If he were devious with the American people, that deviousness can perhaps be justified on the grounds that it was the only path responsible leadership could take in that day. Fully convinced, in the bleak first two years of the forties, that Nazi Germany constituted a threat not only to the survival of democracy itself but also to the physical security of the United States, Roosevelt could only hope that in part by rhetoric but mainly by the force of events the American people would also be led to this conclusion. But he understood, and even sympathized with, the endemic pacificism of this nation, hating war as much as any American in that day or any day. Caught in this dilemma, he charted a course geared to sustaining Britain—fully believing that the survival of America depended upon keeping her frontier on the English Channel. At the same time, knowing that the war effort the United States would eventually be called upon to make would require a unity that was then not existent in American life, he dedicated himself at home to calming the atmosphere as best he could. He hoped, by at times exercising restraint upon the all-out interventionists, to keep disparate groups from flying farther apart.

Although he has sometimes been faulted by historians for an apparently overcautious attitude, derived from an underestimation of public support and an exaggeration of the potency of the congressional opposition, it would appear that Roosevelt took exactly the proper course in the 1939-1941 years. There *was* strong political opposition, evident in the partisan voting pattern of Congress, observable especially in 1939 and the latter months of 1941. As far as public opinion is concerned, it was not a question of underestimating popular support; more to the point, he had a basic understanding of how "to lead public opinion by allowing it to get ahead" of him, in order for the country to achieve as nearly as possible a sense of purpose and unity of spirit. In a bleak and dangerous time the United States had a leader with a fundamental comprehension of social realities in American life. In his fight to preserve the thing he believed in most deeply—this country *and* its democratic way of life—he made perhaps his most significant contribution to the successful outcome of World War II by masterful statesmanship in that most difficult, most critical prewar period of 1939-1941.

G.J.B.

Brookline, Massachusetts
February, 1973

CONTENTS

LEADERSHIP IN CRISIS

1

FDR AND WORLD AFFAIRS:
THE EARLY YEARS

In September 1939 the Second World War broke out in Europe, imperiling more certainly than any previous scourge the continuation of a western civilization painstakingly built over long centuries. Fortunately for the United States and for the cause of world humanism, the times found in President Roosevelt a man and a leader firmly pitted against the forces of destruction then unleashed. With total dedication, with an increasingly selfless devotion, he faced the awesome task of leading a nation in the preservation of its democracy and security in a world gone mad. In a wider sense he became the symbol of freedom, as in his New Deal period he had been the symbol of hope, to the world's masses. The words of a campaign speech of 1936 directed toward a domestic situation were now strangely even more applicable in the foreign policy realm; for Roosevelt's actions in the years 1939-1941 were to confirm that the forces of greed had at last "met their match" and to sustain humanity's hope that they were eventually to meet "their master." At home these were years of sensitive and farsighted leadership. As he had done in the depths of the depression, the President continued to comfort and strengthen a people now faced with another threat to survival, this time from abroad.

During the first six years of his presidency, Roosevelt of necessity expended the major portion of his energy in combating the effects of

3

the depression. It was the year 1939 which marked the beginning of all but total preoccupation with foreign affairs. But even in the earlier period, the President was certainly not unaware of the threat to world peace brewing in Japan and Germany. Without any basic program of action, he continued to hope throughout the early and middle thirties that he might find an opportunity for making an effective personal appeal that would lead to a lessening of international tension. Always maintaining that he was a "realist" in foreign policy, he also thought of himself as internationalist rather than isolationist. One month after his 1933 inauguration, he avowed, in a typical self-description, that he "believe[d] in realistic action on broader lines than the isolationists concede."[1]

Roosevelt had always prided himself on being an internationalist, but there are so many contradictions, or apparent contradictions, in his foreign policy positions along the whole length of his public career prior to the World War II period that historians have tended to question both the nature and extent of his internationalism. There is general agreement that in his very early period he belonged with that group which Arthur M. Schlesinger, Jr. described as existing "before Wilson," meaning before Wilson's concept of a League of Nations, when "the proponents of an active foreign policy had been characteristically nationalists." In this same vein Richard Hofstadter found that as Assistant Secretary of the Navy in the Wilson administration FDR had followed a line that was both "nationalistic and bellicose."[2] This contention is reinforced by Professor Frank Freidel's accounts in his biography of Roosevelt.[3] Admiring both his cousin Theodore and Admiral Mahan, Franklin Roosevelt agreed with their sentiments regarding a large navy, spoke out early and frequently for expansion of the navy, and had advocated American entry into World War I long before Wilson found it necessary to ask for a declaration of war.

Converted later, by Wilson, to his ideal of a League of Nations, Roosevelt campaigned in 1919 and 1920, both before and after his nomination as the Democratic party's vice-presidential candidate in 1920, for American entry into the League. He admitted, though, to having earlier harbored a realist's skepticism of the League as being "merely a beautiful dream, a Utopia."[4]

Until very recently the fairly standard interpretation of Roosevelt's position after the 1920 defeat was that he continued to personally favor international cooperation in the twenties, but because the American people had rejected the League, he temporized in his public statements.[5] In 1965 Robert A. Divine concurred with this view, saying that "as an aspiring politician, [Roosevelt] gradually shifted with the prevailing nationalist sentiment," and "in 1932 political expediency led Roosevelt to repudiate the League of Nations."[6] For hopeful of winning the Democratic nomination in 1932, Roosevelt declared himself against American participation in the League when challenged to do so by the powerful William Randolph Hearst, and eventually he won the support of the Hearst newspapers for his candidacy.

Later, finding no strong personal commitment to the League on Roosevelt's part, Divine reversed his earlier opinion. By 1969 he found that Roosevelt's 1932 position could be taken in all sincerity because "in his own mind he had given up on the League of Nations long before, and thus it was quite easy for him to take the final step when Hearst insisted upon it. He had never shared the intense Wilsonian belief that the League of Nations was the best hope of mankind, and in his typically pragmatic way he had come to view the League as an experiment that failed."[7] Divine's later interpretation harks back to a very early position taken by Professor Hofstadter, who found Roosevelt never greatly enthusiastic, even in his 1920 campaign, about the League. "The League may not end war," FDR had admitted, "but nations demand the experiment."[8] In his New York State Grange speech of February 2, 1932, repudiating the League, Roosevelt stated that it had not lived up to the Wilsonian concept of an instrument for world peace but had degenerated into an agency devoted purely to discussion of European affairs (although this might not have happened, he admitted, had America joined). If these were his beliefs about the League of Nations, then his march away from it appears to us more comprehensible than it did to the disappointed Wilsonian internationalist of that day. Professor Freidel, in his well-researched biography, has speculated that Roosevelt himself may have felt that he was not drastically changing his position in 1932. "Apparently he was convinced," writes Freidel, "that his view had long been one of opposition to American entrance into the League. He ordered a search of newspaper files for the previous six years, hoping to find a public statement of his that he could quote back to Hearst, and thus avoid the charges of opportunism."[9]

It is interesting to note that the League of the thirties has not been immune to the criticism that it was devoted merely to the perpetuation of European world domination at a time when world realities would no longer lend themselves to such a concept. Therefore, it does not necessarily follow that a rejection of American entry into the League in 1932 need be a rejection of internationalism per se. However, since the League of Nations had become a symbol of the internationalists, such a rejection by the presidential candidate has to be interpreted as a blow to the wider concept of internationalism itself. Roosevelt, however, tried to deny that this was happening in a none too convincing letter to Robert Woolley, an influential Democrat and a friend of Colonel House.

I had hoped you would understand. Can't you see that loyalty to the ideals of Woodrow Wilson is just as strong in my heart as it is in yours, — but have you ever stopped to consider that there is a difference between ideals and the methods of attaining them? Ideals do not change, but methods do change with every generation and world circumstance.

Here is the difference between me and some of my fainthearted friends: I am looking for the best modern vehicle to reach the goal of an ideal while they insist on a vehicle which was brand new and in good running order twelve years ago. Think this over! And for heaven's sake have a little faith.[10]

Following Roosevelt into the presidential years, historians have had particular difficulty in describing his position during his first term. Generally they have concluded that his actions for the most part, but not his sentiments, were isolationist and have maintained that this course was dictated by expediency. Roosevelt, most aver, took the line of least resistance and "drifted" with the country's isolationist mood.[11] Yet Robert A. Divine in *Roosevelt and World War II*, published in 1969, asserts that Roosevelt was *at heart* an isolationist during the thirties, brought to that feeling by a hatred of war that he shared with that generation. Therefore Divine sees his presidential actions prompted by a studied and consistent isolationism and based on conviction rather than political expediency. In the same year as Divine's book there appeared the three-volume publication of the President's first-term correspondence in foreign affairs, edited by Edgar B. Nixon, of the Franklin D. Roosevelt Library at Hyde Park. Reviewing the Nixon volumes, Arthur Schlesinger, Jr., commented: " 'Franklin D. Roosevelt and Foreign Affairs' will require, I think, a revision of conventional historical judgments on the foreign policy of his first term. This was not a time of wholehearted and dogmatic isolationism."[12] Thus the interpretative controversy goes on, with historians less and less in agreement about Roosevelt and their latest efforts resulting in ever-widening contradictions in interpretation.

Perhaps for a little while to come there may be only one point on which there can be found a climate of agreement among historians, and that is on Roosevelt's ability to conduct foreign policy. Although even here he comes under indictment, by some, for being the "gifted amateur," yet there is the admission, even by his critics, that he was better equipped than most Presidents to operate in the international sphere. His close friend Sumner Welles, Roosevelt's Undersecretary of State and himself an experienced diplomat, summed up his impression of his chief by saying:

By education and training, by long experience in government, through personal knowledge of Europe and of the lands of the Western Hemisphere, and above all else by an almost intuitive understanding of the great forces which control human relations, Franklin Roosevelt brought to the conduct of American foreign relations more specialized qualifications than those possessed by any President since the days of John Quincy Adams.

The historians Langer and Gleason, although not entirely uncritical of Roosevelt, echo Welles when they say:

Among American Presidents, Franklin D. Roosevelt was certainly one of the best fitted by background, education and experience, as well as by interest and temperament, to understand world conditions and to sense their implications for the national interest and security. His consuming interest in geography and his almost passionate devotion to the Navy were only among the most obvious manifestations of his concern for world affairs.[13]

While historians draw attention to his background, his friends, such as Welles, place equal stress on his intuitive understanding of peoples at home and abroad. Frances Perkins, in her perceptive book, *The Roosevelt I Knew*, finds that one of the strengths in Roosevelt's judgments lay in the fact that he relied upon intuition, that "he had to have feeling as well as thought." Since, as Miss Perkins indicates, he came into contact with and learned to know many different kinds of people, his intuitions were no doubt based on solid knowledge of the workings of human relationships.

A strong factor in Roosevelt's conduct of foreign affairs was his own conception of himself in the presidential office. He felt peculiarly fitted to be President. He was certain, too, as he faced in his own mind the inevitability of America's entry into World War II, that he was the only one who could lead this country successfully through that war.[14] Roosevelt did not belong with the majority of Presidents who have served their terms somewhat in awe of the office.

"The White House was for him almost a family seat . . . ," writes
Richard Neustadt. "Once he became the President of the United
States that sense of fitness gave him an extraordinary confidence.
Roosevelt, almost alone among our Presidents, had no conception of
the office to live up to; he was it. . . . he saw the job of being
President as being F.D.R."[15]

At home in foreign affairs, also sensing himself truly to be the head
of state, it is not surprising that he had a great penchant for personal
diplomacy. He turned often to the thought of meetings between
himself and foreign leaders—Mussolini, Hitler, Konoye, for instance
—as the ideal method by which the growing international problems
of the decade might be tackled and solved. "The evidence is
unmistakable," say Langer and Gleason, "of his great faith in the
efficacy of direct discussion at the highest level, where decisions
could be reached without the intervention of subordinates," and
they attribute "his persistent predilection for personal conferences
with foreign statesmen" to "his sense of exalted position and of his
almost unlimited confidence in his personal influence and ability."[16]

Given to personal diplomacy, Roosevelt made every effort to keep
his channels of information on conditions abroad varied and direct.
Always anxious to supplement official sources, he encouraged friends
in a position to have information to communicate with him directly.
His ambassadors were also under what one of them acknowledged to
be "a special injunction to report directly to you anything I thought
you ought to know. . . ."[17] Although direct communication from
ambassadors was a practice entirely in keeping with the American
institutional structure, Roosevelt was criticized for bypassing the
State Department. He did tend, in the matter of conversations with
his ambassadors, to be careless in failing to make memorandums. He
also encouraged his ambassadors to send him private letters which
they neglected to file with the State Department at the same time.[18]

Department of State and White House records for the decade of
the thirties reveal high-level reporting from official and unofficial
observers abroad. In the two key trouble spots of Berlin and Tokyo
the United States was represented by men of very high caliber,
William E. Dodd and Joseph C. Grew, respectively. Grew, a fellow
Grotonian and a personal friend of Franklin Roosevelt, had been
Hoover's ambassador to Japan and was retained by the new
administration. Although he repeatedly emphasized that care should
be taken not to provoke the militant faction in Japan, and thereby
weaken the moderates on whom he relied to keep the peace, his faith

in the moderates did not influence his reporting. Grew's communications are models of objectivity. In an early report to the State Department, which also found its way to the President, he outlined Japan's fighting strength and said in summary that

... it is my opinion that Japan probably has the most complete, well-balanced, coordinated and therefore powerful fighting machine in the world today. I do not refer to the army only, but to the combination of sea, land and air forces, backed up as they are by enormous reserves of trained men, by industrial units coordinated with the fighting machine and by large reserves of supplies. . . . The machine probably could not stand a protracted, severe war, as industrial supplies would become exhausted, but for a quick, hard push I do not believe that the machine has its equal in the world.

. . .

More than the size of the nation or the strength of its fighting machine, however, the thing which makes the Japanese nation actually so powerful and potentially so menacing, is the national morale and esprit de corps—a spirit which perhaps has not been equalled since the days when the Mongol hordes followed Genghis Khan in his conquest of Asia.

Preceding his description of the Japanese fighting force with a character analysis of the people, Grew described them as "intelligent, industrious, energetic, extremely nationalistic, war-loving, aggressive and, it must be admitted, somewhat unscrupulous." This type of reporting could leave Roosevelt in no doubt as to the potential danger from Japan, although Grew was careful to add that the Japanese, having designs only on the Far East, were a threat to the United States only indirectly in that they "consider the United States as their potential enemy, . . . because they think that the United States is standing in the path of the nation's natural expansion and is more apt to interfere with Japan's ambitions than are the European nations."[19]

Stanley K. Hornbeck, chief of the State Department's Division of Far Eastern Affairs and a pro-China man, thought so highly of Grew's report that he called it to the special attention of Secretary Hull as "one of the most important documents that has come in for a long time."[20] Hornbeck advocated meeting the Japanese threat by a dual policy of friendliness with the Soviet Union and expansion of the United States Navy,[21] the two avenues which the President himself was taking in the early thirties. There has been substantial speculation that Roosevelt's real purpose in recognizing the Soviet Union in 1933 was strategic, that he hoped the Soviets might stand in the way of the expansionist tendencies of Germany and Japan.[22] At the same time, in letters to intimates Roosevelt explained that the naval policy of his first administration was directed towards presenting a strong defense front vis-à-vis Japan. "The Navy program was wholly mine," he informed the Reverend Malcolm E. Peabody, son of his old headmaster at Groton, Endicott Peabody.

Somewhat to my dismay, I discovered that as a simple mathematical problem of self-defense the Japanese had built and kept their Navy up to Treaty provisions. Great Britain had done so in large part but we had not kept up at all, with the net result that our Navy was and probably is actually inferior to the Japanese Navy.

All this I tell you in confidence of course, and also the further fact that the whole scheme of things in Tokio [sic] does not make for an assurance of non-aggression in the future.

As a matter of fact our building program, far from building us up to our Treaty quotas, will barely suffice to keep us almost up to the ship strength of the Japanese Navy and still, of course, far below the British Navy. I am not concerned about the latter, but I am about the first.[23]

Never doctrinaire, Roosevelt's thinking on Japan tended to alter with altering circumstances. During his stint as Assistant Secretary of the Navy he had held that conflict with Japan was probably inevitable. In the mid-twenties, however, in a period of fervent hope for peace, he had written an article for *Asia* in which he had predicted a deadlock if the United States and Japan went to war and had pleaded for greater understanding of Japan. Perhaps it was time, he said, to rethink traditional attitudes. "Although today the Open Door . . . is, with the Monroe Doctrine, the only definitely expressed foreign policy of the United States, we can now recognize that there is a real necessity to Japan of the markets and the raw products of that part of the Chinese mainland contiguous to her island shores. Here, then, is another reason for altering or abandoning the old-fashioned habit of mind."[24]

But following the Japanese attack in Manchuria in 1931, Roosevelt again became concerned about danger from Japan. Referring unceremoniously to "the Japs" in even his earliest press conferences, he was indignant that they should be peace-breakers.[15] In his second cabinet meeting he discussed the possibility of war with Japan.[26] Nevertheless, as the thirties wore on, Roosevelt and his advisers came to feel that the primary threat to peace was from Nazi Germany and Fascist Italy. "Japan is by no means a totalitarian state," Ambassador Grew was reassuring audiences in 1939. Roosevelt, himself, may have had more doubts about freedom of thought in Japan than his ambassador,[27] but neither he nor anyone else could question the totalitarianism of Germany and Italy. Worse yet, they were ruled, as Roosevelt came to believe, by madmen.[28]

As the record shows, although FDR was never in doubt about Hitler, his opinion of Mussolini evolved more slowly. "During the early Mussolini period up through 1932," Roosevelt explained in January 1938,

I very clearly analyzed it as a phenomenon somewhat parallel to the Communist experiment in Russia. . . . It should be remembered that during those years Mussolini still maintained a semblance of parliamentary government, and there were many, including myself, who hoped that having restored order and morale in Italy he would, of his own accord, work toward a restoration of democratic processes.

The question should also be raised as to whether, if Hitler and Nazi-ism had not risen in 1933 and gone to such extreme lengths, Mussolini could have survived alone, could have put through an increasingly greater absolutism, or whether he would have been compelled to reestablish some form of popular representation.[29]

Before Italian aggression in Ethiopia Roosevelt appears to have had some hope that Mussolini might be able to stop Hitler on his march down the road to belligerency. When John S. Lawrence, chairman of the New England Council, suggested that Roosevelt persuade Mussolini to call an international conference and preside over it the President replied: "I don't mind telling you in confidence that I am keeping in fairly close touch with the admirable Italian gentleman." Two months later Roosevelt wrote to his ambassador in Italy, Breckinridge Long, "Signor Mussolini has a wonderful chance to force through an agreement at the Disarmament Conference [which had been meeting in Geneva since 1932]. Frankly, I feel that he can accomplish more than anyone else."[30]

Roosevelt never reached a comparable level of communication or personal understanding with Hitler. Hitler's own ravings, and more especially the religious persecutions in Germany, of which the President was receiving many reports in 1933,[31] may indeed have precluded anything of this sort. When Roosevelt was asked in 1935 about the possibility of sending greetings to the Führer on the occasion of Germany's national holiday, he obviously thought it advisable not to do so, since no message was ever sent.[32] Nevertheless, he continued to look for an opportunity to reach an accord with the dictators, even Hitler. Believing as he did in personal diplomacy, he speculated with intimates in 1936 about persuading world leaders to attend a conference at sea where they might, in the peaceful solitude of ocean, come to an understanding among themselves to prevent war. Even as late as mid-1938 he was still attempting to set up a meeting between himself and Hitler.[33]

With the world situation what it was Roosevelt undoubtedly felt that he must make these attempts. He could hardly have been sanguine about the outcome, however, in view of the fact that he had serious misgivings about both Hitler and the German nation. He knew the Germans to be dangerous because prone to submit unquestioningly to authority and therefore easily led by dictators.[34] When Roosevelt reminisced in later years about his early childhood impressions of Germany—he had been taken abroad for a few months each year by his parents, spending much of the time in Germany, and attended school there for six weeks in 1891—what he recalled most was Germany's militaristic bent under Kaiser Wilhelm II. This early impression was no doubt reinforced, or maybe even crystallized, by the World War I experience. Freidel writes that during the war "Roosevelt's view of the Germans as a monstrous nation grew increasingly grimmer," and that he would have preferred driving "on to Berlin" rather than the granting of an armistice before Germany was invaded. On his trip to Europe in 1919 Roosevelt was distressed to find that the occupying authorities, in order not to offend German sensibilities, were not flying the American flag over the Rhineland fortress Ehrenbreitstein. In this instance, the young Asssistant Secretary of the Navy managed to have rectified what he considered a grave mistake.[35] Already exhibiting a good deal of wisdom in international affairs, he sensed what historians later would emphasize all too knowingly, that Germany should have been made to feel that she had lost the war and only such a lesson would preclude the rise once again of the militaristic spirit in that country.

By the thirties, Franklin Roosevelt's own impressions of Germany were being echoed in correspondence from knowledgeable on-the-spot observers. Samuel R. Fuller, the president of American Bemberg Corporation, who had business connections in Germany and contacts in high places, kept Roosevelt informed about developments there. "To us," wrote Fuller, in a detailed and astute report of May 11, 1933, "it seems also that Germany, a nation which loves to be led, is again a marching nation; and so a danger." George Earle, Minister to Austria, concurred: "Politically the whole situation in Europe centers on Hitler. In my opinion, he is a paranoiac. . . . He has made the militaristic spirit today in Germany the most intense in her history."[36] The reports of Ambassador Dodd and George Messersmith, Consul General in Berlin from 1930 to 1934, left no doubt as to the nature of the leaders of the new Reich,[37] although Dodd, who held a Ph.D. degree from the University of Leipzig, kept insisting that "liberal and intellectual Germany" disapproved of the leadership and hoped for its downfall. "All liberal Germany is with us," he declared, "and more than half of Germany is at heart liberal."[38]

Either through his own sense of men and nations or because of the excellent reporting that he was privy to, Franklin Roosevelt, almost alone among the leaders of the Western democracies, recognized early what Hitler's coming to power meant for Europe and the world. Churchill was still writing, in 1935, in his essay, "Hitler —Monster or Hero?", that "both possibilities are open at the present moment. . . . We must never forget nor cease to hope for the bright alternative."[39] "Roosevelt," declared the former Reichsbank President and Minister of Economics, Dr. Hjalmar Schacht, at the Nuremberg war trials, "was the only one who saw the Hitler administration for what it was from the very beginning, and he was the only one who never sent a representative to a single Party meeting—not one."[40]

During the war the President's good friend Sumner Welles commented:

It is strange now to recollect how lightly the rest of the world accepted this portentous development. It was only very rarely—and, surprisingly enough, least of all in the Foreign Offices of the Western democracies—that Hitler was seen to be the spearhead of the most evil force which had come out of Europe since the conclusion of the first World War and one which—granted the virility, discipline, and military capacity of the German people—would devastate civilization unless it were checked at the outset.[41]

The concluding passage is so reminiscent of Roosevelt's original assessment of German docility under dictators, that it may very well have been Roosevelt speaking. But by the time Welles' book was written, in 1944, the "evil force" of Hitler was at last as evident to the world as it had always been to Franklin Roosevelt.

*　*　*

Through the thirties, as Hitler moved toward his goals of remilitarization of Germany and geographical expansion, Roosevelt, although having of necessity to direct the greater part of his attention to battling the depression at home, took action along whatever narrow lines were open to him in an attempt to stop the Führer. A favorite avenue of approach was to appeal to the dictators on moral grounds. Woodrow Wilson's self-appointed position of spokesman for the peace-loving masses of the world was assumed by Roosevelt, who as the first Democratic President since 1920 had inherited the Wilson mantle. It was a role Roosevelt was particularly well adapted to fill since, as reports from Europe were indicating, he very early caught the imagination of peoples abroad with his courage and confidence and flair for the dramatic, all of which were already resulting in the remarkable legislative record of his first one hundred days.

In the midst of the strenuous hundred day period he gave his attention to trying to save the Geneva Disarmament Conference when it was feared that Hitler intended to proclaim the rearmament of Germany and so sabotage the conference. Roosevelt's method was to send a message to heads of state, on May 16, 1933, which was really intended as an appeal to world public opinion. Its opening sentence stated as much. "A profound hope of the people of my country," the President began, "impels me, as the head of their Government, to address you and, through you, the people of your Nation." Felix Frankfurter, writing to Roosevelt the week before, was enthusiastic about the outcome of this appeal:

I was, and still am, excited by your suggestion of appealing, through the heads of states, to the peoples of Europe to save the Disarmament Conference. There is every reason for hoping that the peoples of Europe will respond, as our people are responding, to an appeal by you. I am confident that the governments of Europe are much more timid and lethargic about daring action than their peoples.[42]

Good democrat that he was, Roosevelt still had some hope, in 1933, about the power of peoples to alter the course of action of governments, and he seems to have guessed correctly. Hitler may very well have been keeping a weather eye on public opinion, for his speech to the Reichstag, scheduled for the next day, May 17, was less belligerent than had been feared. Both Secretary of State Hull and Norman Davis gave Roosevelt credit for the result, but Raymond Moley, then an Assistant Secretary of State, did not think that Hitler had in any way altered his basic position or that Roosevelt had had any effect upon him at all.[43]

By the end of the year Hitler had withdrawn from the Disarmament Conference and the League of Nations, but Roosevelt tried still another appeal along the same lines as his May 16 message. In an address on December 28, to the Woodrow Wilson Foundation, which he had helped create in the twenties, Roosevelt reiterated his reliance on the will of the common man. Declaring that "in every continent and in every country Woodrow Wilson accelerated comprehension on the part of the people themselves," he speculated that "the men and women [certain leaders] serve are so far in advance of that type of leadership that we could get a world accord on world peace immediately if the people of the world could speak for themselves." In this speech the President also expressed a theme that he was beginning to emphasize in his private correspondence, that 10 percent of the world's population, living under dictators, threatened the peace desires by 90 percent. By this time he was not as optimistic as he had been earlier in the year[44] about the 10 percent's chances to change their governments' policies, and he only suggested that "if the 10 percent . . . can be persuaded by the other 90 percent to do their own thinking and not be led, we shall have practical peace, permanent peace, real peace throughout the world."[45]

Roosevelt in such appeals was capitalizing upon America's moral force. But at the same time he went beyond words to an attempt at specific action. At the end of April 1933 he agreed to a suggestion from Norman Davis, chairman of the United States delegation to the Disarmament Conference, that the United States give assurance to nations at the conference, and to France especially, whose fear of German attack was a major obstacle to a disarmament agreement, that if they should find it necessary in the future to designate a nation as an aggressor and to impose sanctions, the United States would refrain from doing anything which might defeat the effectiveness of such action. In effect, this meant the United States would refrain from shipping arms to that nation designated as aggressor. Such a promise would make this country a silent partner to any collective security arrangement undertaken by the powers. To implement this pledge it was necessary that the President have legislative authority to impose an arms embargo on an aggressor nation. A resolution to this effect was already before the Congress, having been initiated by Hoover's Secretary of State, Henry L. Stimson. The House passed it in April. In May, however, the Senate Foreign Relations Committee added an amendment requiring the President to embargo arms shipments to *all* parties to a future war, thus taking discretion away from the President and changing the nature of the original resolution. Although Roosevelt at first agreed to the amendment, Hull finally persuaded him to abandon the resolution altogether, since it was not designed to limit the Executive in his conduct of foreign policy.[46]

Hull had been particularly upset over Roosevelt's initial and easy acceptance of the Foreign Relations Committee amendment. Perhaps domestic considerations had dictated Roosevelt's action. The amendment had been proposed by the powerful senator from California, Hiram Johnson, an irreconcilable in 1919 and still a member of the Foreign Relations Committee in the thirties. Johnson, also an old Progressive, had supported Roosevelt in the 1932 campaign and had rendered much assistance in the West. Equally important, the President still needed his support for passage of New Deal domestic programs.[47]

By no means the isolationist that has sometimes been supposed, Roosevelt had taken a strong moral position in the first months of his presidency and had even entertained the thought of adopting a collective security measure. But words and spasmodic and incomplete action were not enough to stop aggression. Indeed, as the thirties wore on Roosevelt became increasingly apprehensive of the United States' chances to deter the dictators—especially Hitler, who on March 16, 1935 announced German rearmament and restored conscription, in defiance of the Versailles Treaty. Hitler's proclamation prompted Great Britain, France, and Italy to meet shortly thereafter at Stresa, Italy, to consider joint action. On the eve of the Stresa meeting Roosevelt confided to Colonel House his misgivings about the effectiveness of any new appeal from the United States but also revealed that he was still willing for the United States to lend support to a policy of collective security, if the opportunity should arise:

I am, of course, greatly disturbed by events on the other side—perhaps more than I should be. I have thought over two or three different methods by which the weight of America would be thrown into the scale of peace and of stopping the armaments race. I reject each in turn for the principal reason that I fear any suggestion on our part would meet with the same kind of chilly, half-contemptuous reception on the other side as an appeal would have met in July or August, 1914.

I wish you would give some thought, however, to the following, which is based solely on the event of some form of joint military and naval action against Germany. It seems to me that if France, Italy, England and the "Little Entente" decide on positive action they would be far wiser not to invade Germany but rather to establish a complete blockade of Germany. This would involve blockading the Polish, Czecho-Slovak, Austrian, Swiss, French, Belgian, Dutch and Danish borders. The ports of Germany would be taken care of by British Naval operations. . . . If we found it was an effective blockade, as a matter of fact, recognition of the blockade by us would obviously follow. This, after all, is not a boycott nor an economic sanction, but in effect it is the same thing. A boycott or sanction could not be recognized by us without Congressional action but a blockade would fall under the Executive's power after establishment of the fact. I advance this thought because rumor has come to me that something along this line may be discussed at Stresa.[48]

In the same year as the inconclusive Stresa conference the first act of the neutrality legislation of the thirties was passed in the United States. Roosevelt himself, concerned that the United States not be drawn into another world war on technicalities, took the initiative in bringing about the Neutrality Act of 1935. Although he was under no illusions about the United States' chances to stay out of another world war, should one develop—he had stated in his vice-presidential campaign in 1920 that "every sane man knows that in case of another world-war America would be drawn in anyway, whether we were in the League or not"[49] —he wanted to have as much freedom of action as possible. Robert Divine reasons that Roosevelt's "ultimate consideration was to control the future course of American foreign policy. He realized that the United States might eventually enter a European conflict, but he wanted to insure that such a decision would be made on the basis of a careful weighing of national interests rather than in a vain effort to protect the profits of neutral trade."[50] Therefore, when Charles Warren, former Assistant Attorney General under Wilson, suggested, in an article in the April 1934 issue of *Foreign Affairs*, that it would be best for this country to abandon certain traditional neutral rights, Secretary Hull and the President reacted quickly. Warren's article had given what was to become a blueprint for the neutrality legislation of the thirties—recommendations for bans on arms and private loans to belligerents and prohibition of American travel on belligerent ships. As a result, the State Department asked him to prepare a paper on neutrality, which the President requested to see. Soon Roosevelt was writing to the Secretary of State: "This matter of neutral rights is of such importance that I wish you and Phillips and Judge Moore would discuss the whole subject and let me know if you think I should recommend legislation to the coming session of Congress."[51] Roosevelt had been concerned with the question of neutral rights for some time. In the preceding year he had given particular attention to a memorandum by J. Pierrepont Moffat, chief of the

State Department's Division of Western European Affairs. Moffat had written that "two of our wars have been fought on the issue of the maintenance of our neutral rights. If . . . we can avoid similar dangers in the future, we stand to be the gainer"; Roosevelt had underlined the phrase "maintenance of our neutral rights."[52] By 1935 he was so anxious for some action along the lines suggested by the Warren study that, while meeting with Nye committee members in March of that year, he suggested, rather unexpectedly, that they apply themselves to a subject they had not thought of at all—neutrality legislation. Since the State Department was already tackling the same question, Secretary Hull was decidedly agitated by Roosevelt's latest move. It was, however, a common Rooseveltian administrative practice to set up overlapping jurisdictions and have two different groups working on the same problem. In this case it was all the more necessary because the State Department, split into two camps on the issue of discretionary versus impartial embargo, was making very little headway.[53] Out of the inevitable confusion that Roosevelt had now created, finally came the first Neutrality Act, signed by the President on August 31, 1935.

The act required the President "upon the outbreak or during the progress of war between, or among, two or more foreign states" to impose an impartial arms embargo against all parties to the war. It gave him authority to declare, at his discretion, that travel by American citizens on belligerent ships would be at their own risk. The act also contained a provision creating a National Munitions Control Board, considered very important by the administration, since it gave the government licensing control over exports of arms.

Pleased with the greater part of the legislation, Roosevelt was upset enough with its major provision—the indiscriminate arms embargo —to strengthen Cordell Hull's draft of a statement to be released by the President upon signing the joint resolution. "It is conceivable that situations may arise in which inflexible provisions of law might have exactly the opposite effect from that which was intended," Hull had written. To this, Roosevelt added, "In other words, the inflexible provisions might drag us into war instead of keeping us out."[54]

The President had hoped for a discretionary embargo, and was only willing to sign the Neutrality Act of 1935 because he realized that in the case of the impending Italian-Ethiopian war the inflexible embargo would work against the aggressor Italy, the country with the navy and financial resources. In order to guarantee that it would apply only to the Ethiopian war, he asked for and obtained a six-months expiration clause for the section of the act containing the arms embargo provision.[55] Trying to make the most of an imperfect situation, Roosevelt wrote to Ambassador Dodd, "Meanwhile, the country is being fairly well educated, and I hope that next January I can get an even stronger law, leaving, however, some authority to the President."[56]

An isolationist Congress, however, was not about to give the President "an even stronger law." A precedent had been established, and subsequent neutrality acts, one in 1936 and the permanent Neutrality Act of May 1, 1937, retained the mandatory arms embargo while adding new features. The 1936 act established a ban on loans to belligerents, and the 1937 act allowed the President at his discretion to place trade with belligerents in goods other than arms and implements of war on a cash-and-carry basis. This assured that there would be no American ships engaged in belligerent trade. In addition, the 1937 act prohibited the arming of U.S. merchant ships. By 1937, with more hindsight than foresight, Congress had attempted to take care of every factor which was presumed to have been a cause for American entry into World War I. The 1937 law was ridiculed by the *New York Herald-Tribune* as "an act to preserve the United States from intervention in the War of 1914-18."[57]

As much as Roosevelt disliked the mandatory arms embargo feature in all the neutrality legislation, he found many parts of the legislation of 1935-1937 advisable. There are evidences that Roosevelt himself, whose New Deal rhetoric is studded with derogatory references to bankers, had begun to feel that the activities of bankers and munitions makers may have had much to do with United States entry into World War I. "He had been influenced by parts of the revisionist interpretation," writes Warren Cohen, in his historiographical study of World War I revisionism.[58] For one who had chafed under the pacifism of Secretary of State Bryan and his own chief in the Navy Department, Secretary Daniels, in the days before American entry into World War I, it was with a complete about face that Roosevelt, impressed with Nye committee revelations about the munitions industry, wrote to Daniels in October 1934, "Would that W.J.B. have stayed on as Secretary of State—the country would have been better off."[59] He even conceded that U.S. entry into World War I might have been avoided. To Oswald Garrison Villard of *The Nation* he wrote: "You are right in part about President Wilson. The difficulty is that in those days most people were thinking in terms of the old international law which is now completely disappeared. From the point of view of hindsight, we might have kept out, but at the time we were following the precedents of several centuries."[60] No longer following the "precedents of several centuries" Roosevelt was just as willing as the American public in the thirties to see the neutrality acts incorporate restrictions on the traditional rights of neutral trade. The Democratic party's foreign policy plank in 1936, drafted in the White House by Roosevelt's friend William C. Bullitt, stated unequivocally: "We shall continue . . . to work for peace and to take the profits out of war; to guard against being drawn, by political commitments, international banking or private trading, into any war which may develop anywhere."[61]

In like degree Roosevelt shared with the public its hatred of war, the terror at the heart of the isolationist sentiment of the thirties. There was a time when the youthful Roosevelt, according to his biographer Professor Freidel, was "fascinated rather than repelled" in his 1918 mid-summer tour of World War I battlefields, "thrilled by the patriotism and heroism of the American and Allied troops, and oppressed by a sense of guilt and deprivation because he was not sharing their vicissitudes." This scarcely sounds like the same man who, in one of his more passionate speeches, the Chautauqua address in August 1936, uttered the following words:

I have seen war. I have seen war on land and sea. I have seen blood running from the wounded. I have seen men coughing out their gassed lungs. I have seen the dead in the mud. I have seen cities destroyed. I have seen two hundred limping, exhausted men come out of line—the survivors of a regiment of one thousand that went forward forty-eight hours before. I have seen children starving. I have seen the agony of mothers and wives. I hate war.

I have passed unnumbered hours, I shall pass unnumbered hours, thinking and planning how war may be kept from this Nation.

William C. Bullitt, the diplomat whom Roosevelt had appointed first Ambassador to the Soviet Union, now assisting him in his campaign for reelection, had drafted the speech. The sentiments were so much those of the President, however, that his Christmas gift that year to close friends was an inscribed copy of the Chautauqua address.[62]

Friends have testified to the great change in Roosevelt's personality that came with his affliction, infantile paralysis. Stricken in the summer of 1921, at age 39, he was never to walk unaided again. A tragedy of this magnitude is bound to change any man's outlook, for better or for worse. His old friend William Phillips, who had known him since his first days in Washington, as Assistant Secretary of the Navy, found that polio had deepened Roosevelt and strengthened him, given him the elements of greatness which he had not possessed before undertaking his gigantic and patient struggle to overcome his affliction. Frances Perkins wrote:

Franklin Roosevelt underwent a spiritual transformation during the years of his illness. I noticed when he came back that the years of pain and suffering had purged the slightly arrogant attitude he had displayed on occasion before he was stricken. The man emerged completely warmhearted, with humility of spirit and with a deeper philosophy. Having been to the depths of trouble, he understood the problems of people in trouble.[63]

It is not unreasonable to suppose, therefore, that Roosevelt's changed attitude toward war was due, in part, to the change in his own personality. When he thought of the effects of war, he thought in terms of the killing, in terms of lives lost and bodies maimed.[64] One is struck, in listening to recordings of the war speeches, with the surge of sympathy in his voice whenever he spoke of the war dead. Although he never lost his innate optimism and was as far from having a tragic view of life as anyone could be, yet he had developed the capacity truly to understand personal tragedy by the time he became President.

When Professor Divine, in *Roosevelt and World War II*, terms Roosevelt an isolationist, he sees the President's hatred of war as the basis for his supposedly isolationist predilections. Divine interprets the Chautauqua speech, a major foreign policy address in a campaign year, as entirely sincere and therefore much more than simple good politics. That it was also politically wise, no one could deny. The age was isolationist, and the President was speaking the majority sentiment exactly. But even in the Chautauqua speech he added the realistic warning, "Yet we must remember that so long as war exists on earth there will be some danger that even the Nation which most ardently desires peace may be drawn into war."

Much too aware of power relationships in the world to believe that the United States could escape the impact of widespread aggression, Roosevelt nevertheless, with some amount of inconsistency, adopted a variety of policies in the thirties. Accustomed as he was to what he had called in an accurate self-analysis "playing it by ear," it would appear that his approach to foreign policy was to rely on instinct and let the event of the moment dictate the best course to follow. Even if he had wanted to lend himself to a strong policy of collective security, he was hampered not only by the Congress at home but by the indecisiveness of the European democracies. Even Robert Divine, critical as he is of United States isolationism in the thirties, indicts Britain and France for failure to take effective action against the aggressor during the Ethiopian conflict and the reoccupation of the Rhineland in 1936. Divine contends:

A strong stand by the western democracies might have permitted Roosevelt to offer American support, but British and French appeasement compelled the United States to seek security by insulating itself from Europe. The European appeasers were in a very real sense the co-authors of American neutrality policy.[65]

In the fall of 1937, however, Roosevelt determined to make a stronger effort to save the peace of the world. With aggression developing once more in Asia and the European situation deteriorating badly, he reacted to Hull's suggestion that the time had come to try to restrain the growth of American isolationism.[66] The result was the Quarantine speech of October 5 in which Roosevelt, now firmly emphasizing that there could be no safety in an American storm cellar if a world were at war, attempted to alert the public and to start it thinking in a new, nonisolationist direction.[67] Interpreting public reaction to the speech as highly unfavorable[68] —he later said to Judge Rosenman, "It's a terrible thing to look over your shoulder when you are trying to lead—and to find no one there,"[69] —Roosevelt did not attempt another public appeal for another year and a half. American diplomacy during that time was also not very aggressive. At the same time, the European situation remained somewhat fluid. War was averted at Munich, and the President was "momentarily optimistic," Langer and Gleason find. Shortly after Munich, however, it became obvious to him that a second world war was in the making,[70] and he could at last face a concrete situation.

Hitler and the Japanese militarists had acted as terrible simplifiers. Japan had resumed aggression in China in 1937. Since Japan was already a party to a defensive alliance with Germany, the Anti-Comintern Pact of November 25, 1936, if Hitler now moved at any time decisively against the West, it was not unlikely that Japan would be spurred to attacks on the colonial areas of the Far East. With the outbreak of new and more virulent persecutions against the Jews in Germany in November 1938 ("I myself could scarcely believe that such things could occur in a twentieth century civilization," said Roosevelt),[71] it was becoming evident that Hitler anticipated further crimes against civilization. The United States recalled its ambassador to Germany, Hugh Wilson, for "consultation," and he was never sent back. A few weeks earlier, and almost immediately after Munich, Hitler had announced further rearmament. At the end of 1938 the war in Europe, which had been anticipated for so long, seemed close at hand, and for Roosevelt the situation had crystallized. His actions would now become more precise, his policies more consistent, as he turned from depression problems and gave his full attention to battling the terrible simplifiers now threatening to usher in a new dark age.

2

NEW DIRECTIONS

Never a bona fide isolationist at any stage of his presidency, Roosevelt nevertheless floundered in the uncertain climate of the mid-thirties, at a loss to know just what he could do. Even Europeans anxious to have America take the lead against the aggressors had no positive suggestions for the United States. As Bullitt, the newly appointed ambassador to France, reported to Roosevelt in 1936, "every minister of a small European state who has yet called on me has expressed the hope that you might intervene." But when he asked how the President could intervene, what he could do to prevent war, Bullitt continued, "the reply invariably has been that no one in Europe can think of any way in which you can intervene effectively—but you might be able to think of some way yourself."[1]

Not until the post-Munich days, when he sensed the imminence of war in Europe, did Roosevelt's foreign policy crystallize and take direction. For a year before, however, the beginnings of a new and different course of action can be detected, although at the same time the President continued in the old mold of spasmodic diplomatic attempts to stem the tide of aggression abroad, and at home, after the Quarantine speech, he said very little to the public in the way of warning.

The year 1938, however, saw an added ingredient in presidential policy. The President began to turn his attention to certain aspects of rearmament, specifically naval preparedness and airplane production.

24

The concern for the navy was occasioned by manifestly aggressive tendencies on the part of Japan, which was also, by the fall of 1937, linked in a loose alliance structure with both Italy and Germany. Although the navy was in much better condition than the army, due in part to Roosevelt's own interest and to his having pushed a naval building program in his early years in office, there was still much to be done to put the navy on a competitive basis vis-à-vis the aggressor nations. Determined by 1938 to build a two-ocean fleet large enough to equal the combined power of the navies of Germany, Italy, and Japan, Roosevelt, on January 28, sent a special message to Congress calling for rearmament and emphasizing naval expansion. There was strong isolationist opposition, but after long and hard debate, Congress in that year passed the Vinson Naval Expansion Act, giving the President substantially what he had asked for. The act called for great increases in naval strength—twenty-four new battleships and equivalent increases in smaller craft—and also small gains for the army and air corps.[2]

Roosevelt also evidenced interest in airplane production in 1938. The first indication of this new interest can be seen in his giving personal attention to the French air missions that were sent to the United States that year to place orders with private American manufacturers. Since 1938 was the year Hitler effected the Anschluss with Austria and next raised the Sudeten question, which, for a time, threatened Europe with general war, the French were beginning to feel very pressured. Worried that their aircraft production was considerably behind German production, they began to place orders in the United States. Roosevelt personally supervised French plane purchases here, and even after he later formally assigned to Secretary of the Treasury Henry Morgenthau, Jr., on December 17, 1938, the responsibility for foreign munitions orders, the President continued to take an active part in supervising arrangements and determining policy. Two months after the outbreak of the Second World War, Roosevelt wrote Bullitt as follows, in regard to French and, by then, British war-supply purchases:

All that you have done has been excellent and explicit and the only trouble is that the dear British and French Governments are failing, as usual, to be definite between themselves and to be definite to me.

. . .

In regard to purchasing, I am ready to handle the whole matter over here if we only knew whom we were talking to. Our objective is the practical one of not interfering with our own military and naval program and, secondly, to prevent prices from rising in this country.[3]

A word might be said about the Morgenthau appointment, significant in itself for understanding Rooseveltian attitudes. The War Department resented Roosevelt's putting Morgenthau in charge of foreign muitions purchases, but the interpreter of the Morgenthau Diaries, John Blum, justifies the appointment on the grounds of "the uncooperative attitude of the War Department" and declares that "Roosevelt also considered the Treasury's Procurement Division the only agency capable of coordinating French purchases with the requests of both the Army and the Navy."[4] Another reason for the appointment, perhaps more important, was Roosevelt's feeling that he could trust Morgenthau, an old and loyal friend, to carry out the President's own policies. As the letter to Bullitt cited above reveals, with the appointment of Morgenthau Roosevelt by no means relinquished control over foreign purchases but kept all policy-making apparatus in his own hands.

It was toward the end of 1938, in the post-Munich days, that what had been Roosevelt's initial concern with French air missions expanded into a new concentration on the general question of ground and especially air force rearmament for the United States. The President emphasized these matters in a press conference on October 14, 1938, in which he mentioned a long conference he had had the previous evening with Ambassador Bullitt, recently returned from France. The new U.S. fears were prompted by fears abroad. Cognizant of thinking in French official circles, for his relations with French governmental figures were on a strongly personal and intimate basis, the ambassador had described the increasingly strong French concern with German air power. Reports of the same kind were coming to Roosevelt from Britain as well.[5] Munich had at last taught the western democracies the necessity of preparedness. Bullitt had been among the first to have recognized this necessity and had written to Roosevelt just prior to the portentous Munich meeting:

You may be sure that I will come home as soon as I feel I can, as I am dead tired. Meanwhile the prospects for Europe are so foul that the further we keep out of the mess the better.

The moral is: If you have enough airplanes you don't have to go to Berchtesgaden.[6]

Roosevelt's agreement with this line of reasoning is revealed in the President's confidential statement about Munich a few months later to his old friend, Josephus Daniels, then ambassador to Mexico. Daniels' lengthy longhand notes, scribbled immediately after his conversation with Roosevelt, disclose the processes of the President's thought. Recorded Daniels:

In a long talk at the White House with Prest [*sic*] Roosevelt today he told me that an intercepted German order addressed to Ambassador Ribbentrop contained specific plans for an air-raid attack by Germans on London before the Munich meeting—Germany and Italy had 13,000 effective combat planes. The German plan was to begin the attack at 11 o'clock at night with 100 planes and send 100 additional ones every hour to bomb London. The British saw they had power to ward off the first 2 or 3 attacks, but their ammunition [?] and resources could not resist after the first 500 German bombing planes. This knowledge made Chamberlain capitulate at Munich. FDR also said that there was nothing to the talk that the Germans were undernourished, to the contrary the trained German fighting men were strong and in the pink of condition. I did not ask FDR from whom he obtained this information which he accepted as accurate, but as he had recently talked with Ambassadors Kennedy of Britain, Bullitt from France, and Wilson from Germany I am quite sure that was the source of the information which has evidently been fully accepted by him.

Prior to the Munich Conference Roosevelt, upon receiving word of Chamberlain's agreement to meet with Hitler, had cabled his laconic, often cited message, "Good man." The outcome at Munich had momentarily relieved Roosevelt, and Daniels goes on to show why:

When I expressed some doubt as to the great superiority of the totalitarian countries, he said he was so convinced of its accuracy that if he had been in Chamberlain's place he would have felt constrained to have made terms to prevent the war for which Germany was fully prepared. He remarked he could not understand how Britain and France could have permitted themselves to get in such comparative weak position.[7]

Now very anxious about unpreparedness in the western democracies, especially after Hitler's post-Munich announcement of further rearmament and his undertaking of more virulent religious persecutions, Roosevelt began to concentrate in earnest on United States plane production and especially on the expansion of facilities for producing planes. In an important meeting with his military and civilian advisers on November 14, 1938 he presented his idea of what was needed to put the defenses of the United States in readiness. The military were concerned that it was not an integrated program which the President outlined, but one which emphasized airplanes to the exclusion of other considerations. The President was ignoring the building of an air force per se, which would have entailed concentration on pilots, crews, maintenance units, and supply elements. Roosevelt is reputed to have said that he wanted planes to "impress Hitler" and that he could not do this with "barracks and runways, but only with planes." Yet one participant in the November 14 conference, and in subsequent conferences, Major General James H. Burns, came away with the distinct feeling that the President was not increasing American production facilities in order to acquire planes for our own air forces but in order to serve the needs of France and Britain, that what he had in mind was the building up of British and French air power either to deter Hitler or, in the event of war, to enable them to defeat Hitler without the necessity of the United States sending its own armed forces overseas.[8]

Whatever Roosevelt had in mind, it is clear that as he sensed the imminence of the Second World War he began to move with more certainty, direction, and purpose. Rearmament coupled with expansion of production facilities here would put the United States in a better position to throw its weight into the scales when that war broke out. But if the primary purpose of production planning was to aid France and Britain, Roosevelt felt he could not say this directly to the American public, that the times would not allow him to do so. Earlier in the thirties, in the midst of a battle over United States entry into the World Court, he had observed to former Secretary of State Henry L. Stimson, "These are not normal times; people are jumpy and very ready to run after strange gods."[9] Therefore, when in his budget messages of January 5 and January 12, 1939 he called for rearmament, emphasizing the navy and planes, he was circumspect in giving all the reasons for the administration's first strong public concentration on these matters. He stressed that an American expeditionary force to Europe was by no means intended, which was true. Indeed, there has been considerable speculation that as late as September 1941 Roosevelt was still thinking that if America entered the war its contribution could be pretty much limited to massive naval and air power.[10] But he also said that the preparations now being made were solely for defense of these shores, and here was a subterfuge of sorts, designed to insure ready public acceptance. Air power had a particular appeal in that day, and the program was favorably received.[11]

On January 23, however, the public heard a disquieting news report. One of the newest American bombers had crashed in California with an official of the French Air Ministry on board. In the subsequent furor raised by isolationists in and out of Congress,

Roosevelt was forced to acknowledge publicly that he himself had authorized the selling of planes to France. He then met, on January 31, with members of the Senate Military Affairs Committee to explain his policy, in particular to give assurance that the United States had not entered into a secret alliance with France. When after the meeting one or more committee members told the press that the President had made a statement to the effect that the American "frontier was on the Rhine," Roosevelt was furious. In a press conference a few days later he angrily denied the remark, calling it a "deliberate lie. " He also issued a statement of policy which began, "We are against any entangling alliances, obviously." It would appear that with this statement the public was reassured enough even to approve the sale of planes to Britain and France. The Gallup poll in mid-February recorded a healthy 65 percent in favor.[12]

Roosevelt was thinking in terms of defense at a distance but this could not be explained, he felt, to the American people at this time. There were too many vocal isolationists ready to pounce on such explanations, to utilize and perhaps distort them in order to stir up adverse public reaction to presidential policies. Later, during the blitzkrieg of 1940, he made a full statement to the Business Advisory Council, acknowledging that he had predicted war to the Senate Military Affairs Committee in January 1939 and had said "not that 'our frontier was on the Rhine' but that the continued existence of, for example, Finland, or the Baltic States, or the Scandinavian nations—their continued existence as independent nations did have a pretty definite relationship to the defenses of the United States. And there was a most awful howl of protest all over the country, as you know, at that time." And, he continued,

We have to look ahead to certain possibilities. If I had said this out loud in a fireside talk, again people would have said that I was perfectly crazy: The domination of Europe, as we all know, by Naziism—including also the domination of France and England—takes what might be called the buffer out of what has existed all these years between those new schools of government and the United States. The buffer has been the British Fleet and the French Army. If those two are removed, there is nothing between the Americas and those new forces in Europe.[13]

Preparing for war in early 1939, the President faced as his primary task the necessity to seek repeal of the arms embargo, for if that were not accomplished England and France would be immediately stopped from obtaining war supplies here upon the outbreak of conflict. But the embargo had been a central part of the neutrality laws since 1935, and repeal would constitute a major reversal in American foreign policy. Again Roosevelt presented the issue to the people indirectly and with considerable circumspection, not even mentioning repeal of the arms embargo in so many words, but implying a call for repeal with the following passage in his annual message of January 1939:

Words may be futile, but war is not the only means of commanding a decent respect for the opinions of mankind. There are many methods short of war, but stronger and more effective than mere words, of bringing home to aggressor governments the aggregate sentiments of our own people.

At the very least, we can and should avoid any action, or any lack of action, which will encourage, assist or build up an aggressor. We have learned that when we deliberately try to legislate neutrality, our neutrality laws may operate unevenly and unfairly—may actually give aid to an aggressor and deny it to the victim. The instinct of self-preservation should warn us that we ought not to let that happen any more.[14]

After opening the issue of repeal with these introductory remarks, Roosevelt himself remained silent. The administration did not press the case for repeal but readily accepted the offer of Key Pittman, chairman of the Senate Foreign Relations Committee, to initiate the matter in Congress and take responsibility for following through to the achievement of legislation. Roosevelt declined to make further public statements. When asked at a press conference on January 17 what he had meant by "methods short of war," he skirted the question, saying "nobody could ever answer that question ... categorically. ..."[15]

Although a bill for Pittman to introduce was drafted in the State Department,[16] the administration felt it necessary to remain in the background for a number of reasons. Polls after Munich were indicating some changes in public attitudes, but isolationism was still a formidable force in the country. At the same time, Roosevelt's prestige was at an all-time low because of his attempt to "pack" the Supreme Court early in his second term, the 1937-1938 recession, and his attempted purge of conservatives within the Democratic party in the 1938 primaries. Cries of "dictator" mingled with cries of "warmonger," the latter having been inspired by his Quarantine speech. A low-keyed approach appeared advisable and this strategy plus the accumulation of events in the post-Munich period resulted in a favorable public reaction in support of presidential policy. Whereas in September 1938 a Gallup poll had recorded 66 percent opposed to selling arms to either side in the event of war, in February and March of 1939 the polls showed a majority now anxious to help England and France in case of war and favoring repeal of the arms embargo.[17]

Even if public opinion were changing, however, opinions in Congress, and certainly the opinions of the staunch isolationists, were not. The newly elected 76th Congress was Roosevelt's biggest problem at this time and his chief reason for not becoming personally involved in the fight for new legislation. Some of the best-known congressional figures—Senators Borah, Nye, Hiram Johnson, Burton K. Wheeler, for instance—were inveterate isolationists, the "irreconcilables," as Roosevelt termed them. In addition, the anti-Roosevelt forces were greatly strengthened by the elections of 1938. While the Democrats still retained control of the House and Senate, the election had increased Republican representation considerably. The Republicans had gained eighty-one House seats and eight Senate seats, thus adding numbers to the bipartisan anti-New Deal, conservative coalition that had been forming in Congress against Roosevelt since the fall of 1937.[18] Although the conservatives and the isolationists were not necessarily one and the same, at least not as early as 1939 (for, before the blitzkrieg of 1940 the old progressive element was still evident in isolationist ranks),[19] it is true that the Republican congressional party tended toward isolationism. About one-fourth of the Democrats in Congress could also be termed isolationist. When this isolationist strength was coupled with Republican consciousness that they were less than two years away from the next presidential election and hopeful of ousting the New Dealers at last, strategy dictated to the Republicans that they take advantage of the momentary weakness of Roosevelt's own political position and step up their attacks on his foreign policy. It was hardly likely they would go along with the President's plea, voiced time and time again, that "politics stop at the water line."

The strongest weapon at their command was to brand the President a warmonger. An old friend, Cornelius Vanderbilt, Jr., reported that this was precisely what they were doing in early 1939. "The Republicans are spreading a nasty lie to effect, that the President is trying to involve us in war, to re-elect himself," Vanderbilt informed Roosevelt's private secretary Marguerite LeHand.[20] Such a charge was political dynamite. Although public feeling may have been changing in regard to aid to Britain and France and repeal of the arms embargo, the desire to stay out of war remained firm. During the entire period before Pearl Harbor it was the most persistent and most intense feature of American thought, the point on which the greatest numbers registered agreement. The polls of this period bear out Adolf Berle's conviction that the American nation was "endemically pacifist." At the time of the Munich crisis 95 percent were opposed to American participation in another war. Although this percentage was reduced somewhat in the polls of February and March 1939 and drastically reduced just after the outbreak of the European war in September, when a blitzkrieg in the West was expected momentarily, the figure by October was back to its 1938 proportions. In the months before Pearl Harbor it was still strikingly high, with approximately 70 percent against an American declaration of war on the Axis at that time.[21]

In the inauspicious atmosphere of early 1939 Roosevelt's sixth sense told him that this was the time to be as inconspicuous as possible. The noticeable lack of strong statements from the White House came under criticism by some internationalists who wanted the President to exert a more forceful leadership. Thus Professor Clyde Eagleton of New York University wrote to Stanley K. Hornbeck on February 16, 1939:

[The] American people have been confused through irresponsible leadership and ... would welcome a clear statement, and would follow it with relief. In various meetings we discussed this, and everywhere I have found this belief. And when I ask who could furnish such leadership, the answer is always: "Only the President could do it; if only he would give a fireside chat!"[22]

Not all observers were so critical. Some saw in the President's foreign policy a certain direction and clarity at last . One observer noted, "It seems to me that this is the first time within my recollection that the United States has had a foreign policy which could be put on paper."[23] Roosevelt himself agreed with this last estimate, as can be seen in a letter he received in late March from a Treasury Department official, saying:

You may recall that at dinner the other evening we discussed how strange it seemed that the press had failed to realize in its editorial comment the full significance of your foreign policy, and the effect of America's first strong foreign policy on world opinion. You will be interested to note the enclosed radio broadcast conducted by the Christian Science Monitor on March 21. At least one Boston paper realizes.[24]

Judge Rosenman finds Roosevelt "finally committed to a program of collective security."[25] Underlying this gigantic reversal of emphasis in foreign affairs was Roosevelt's own awareness of the threat Hitler posed to the Western Hemisphere, philosophically, economically, strategically. Not yet ready to explain this threat in his public addresses, he was beginning to reveal his thought to members of his official family and, privately, to the press.[26] Roosevelt's habit of thinking was always in terms of world geographical possibilities. In his January conversation with Josephus Daniels he had expressed his concern that Germany might be able to stage an invasion of the Western Hemisphere through Brazil. Daniels recorded:

FDR, speaking of our obligations under the Monroe Doctrine indicated that the first danger to us could [or would?] come from Brazil. I asked if it was because there were nearly a million Germans in Brazil. He answered "There are a million and a half." When ready to send armadas of bombing planes from Africa (look how Africa juts out on the map) is [*sic*] ready to fly to Brazil, a civil war will be started there and German planes will swoop down from Africa on Brazil to decide the war in favor of the side the Germans have taken in the civil war. He spoke as if that might be the real danger to this continent.[27]

In the same vein, at a White House dinner for the American Society of Newspaper Editors held on April 20, Roosevelt stated his belief that Germany and Italy

have somewhere around 1500 planes which can leave their countries tonight, be in the Cape Verde Islands tomorrow morning and be in Brazil tomorrow afternoon. We have eighty planes that could get there in time to meet them. They have 1500. . . . They cannot hop them directly across our 3,000 miles but they can do it in three hops, middle Europe, Cape Verde, Brazil, Yucatan and Tampico. I think I am a lot safer on the Hudson River than I would be if I were in Kansas. They (in Kansas) are awfully close to Mexico. . . .

And, commenting on the recent American fleet maneuvers in the Caribbean, which he himself had attended, the President asserted that it "shows the problems of modern warfare and it shows how terribly close Europe is to the United States."[28]

When Roosevelt spoke at this meeting of the possibility of supplies going from the United States to the European democracies in the event of war, he was asked if the totalitarian nations might not take revenge on the United States if the democracies were eventually defeated. His reply was: "I do not think it would make very much difference. I think if they won the war they would put a Chinese Wall around us anyway." He had explained this concept at a cabinet meeting a few months previously when, as Ickes recorded, the President pointed out, Hitler will not have to control all of Europe and South America in order to make it difficult for us economically. For instance, the Argentine now exports eighty percent of her products to Germany and other European countries. If Hitler can dominate the major part of Europe, he can serve notice on the Argentine that unless it accepts fascist principles and yields to fascistic economic domination, all of her exports to Europe will be cut off.... And the same situation would exist with respect to other South American countries. They could be turned against us and we, in spite of our wealth and resources, would be powerless to do anything except to retire within our own territory, there to get along as best we could. Of course, Canada will necessarily have to throw her fate in with us because she will be cut off from Great Britain and the other members of the British Commonwealth.[29]

While Roosevelt thought and spoke in terms of the variety of methods by which the Nazis could achieve world domination, he tended to emphasize over and over again the possibility of an actual invasion of this hemisphere. Although isolationists then, and revisionist historians later, discounted a Nazi invasion as an absurdity,[30] Roosevelt felt it would be the next step once Hitler gained dominant control of Europe and Atlantic bases. This must not happen, American frontiers must be kept on the Rhine, and repeal of the arms embargo was an essential ingredient for maintaining the Rhine boundary.

Key Pittman was a disappointing procrastinator, however, and from January to April there was virtually no progress on changing the Neutrality Act. The administration became increasingly impatient. When Hitler absorbed Czechoslovakia in mid-March, Roosevelt finally felt compelled to break silence on the repeal issue. Two days after the Czechoslovakian take-over, in a press conference on March 17, the President went on record as follows:

Q Mr. President, do you want a revision of the neutrality legislation this session?
THE PRESIDENT: Put the question a little bit differently: "Do we need legislation on neutrality at this session." The answer is, "Yes."
Q What sort of legislation?
THE PRESIDENT: That we are not talking about at this time.
Q Will you recommend that? Are you going to send a special message?
THE PRESIDENT: I doubt it. I think it can be done at conference.
Q Do you think the developments of the last few days in Europe demonstrate the need for neutrality legislation?
THE PRESIDENT: Yes.[31]

The Pittman bill was finally introduced in the Senate on March 20, becoming one of thirty-three neutrality measures then before Congress. When Pittman's bill became bogged down a second time, in committee hearings, the administration went to Congressman Sol Bloom, chairman of the House Foreign Affairs Committee, for an alternative measure. It was expected that the House would cause fewer problems than the Senate, but when John M. Vorys, Republican representative from Ohio, proposed an amendment to the Bloom bill partially restoring the arms embargo, the House accepted the amendment on a close vote of 159 to 157. Defeated, the administration turned to Pittman again, prevailing upon him to convene his committee and attempt to have his bill reported out. After further procrastination, Pittman complied. But then, on July 11, the Senate Foreign Relations Committee, by a vote of 12 to 11, decided to postpone consideration of neutrality legislation until the next session of Congress.[32]

During these months Roosevelt and State Department officials had worked quietly behind the scenes, holding talks with congressmen. But Roosevelt, preferring to remain in the background, had let Hull make whatever formal public pronouncements were deemed necessary. Once or twice, however, at a press conference, he did speak out for new neutrality legislation, first at the March 17 press conference and next on June 20, at a time when the Bloom bill was under consideration in the House. In response to a reporter's query about whether he wanted action on neutrality legislation before Congress adjourned, Roosevelt replied that he did "for the obvious reason that if, after Congress goes home, some war should start we would find it very difficult to change legislation to create neutrality without having it said that we were favoring one side or the other. For the sake of Congress, it is much easier to insure against getting into that kind of dilemma."[33]

Up to this point, Roosevelt had been indicating in his public and private statements his own expectation of and anxiety about war in Europe. So much had the possibility been on his mind that he had quipped upon leaving Warm Springs on April 9 : "I'll be back in the autumn if we don't have a war." Perhaps politically unsound—the isolationists had immediately taken up the remark as warmongering and created a large stir of protest for a time—Roosevelt's words, whether inadvertent or intended as a warning, do reveal his apprehension about the international situation.

Knowing how unprepared Britain and France were, his wish was to place the United States beforehand in a position to aid the European democracies. He had become all the more anxious about military discrepancies between the democracies and the Axis powers when

Hitler had gained the armament-producing facilities of Czechoslovakia in mid-March. Senator Tom Connally, a member of the
Senate Foreign Relations Committee and a Roosevelt supporter,
reported that

the day after the Germans crossed into Czechoslovakia, F.D.R. asked me to visit
him at the White House. He was in a bad humor and cursed the Neutrality Act.
"If Germany invades a country and declares war, we'll be on the side of Hitler
by invoking the act," he said angrily. "If we could·get rid of the arms embargo,
it wouldn't be so bad."[34]

The whole argument for repeal of the embargo had been that it was
necessary in ordeι to aid the allies. At his April 20 meeting with the
American Society of Newspaper Editors, Roosevelt had spoken of "a
fifty-fifty chance there will be a war in Europe," and also a fifty-fifty
chance as to who would win the war. This had brought the following
exchange:

Q If this fifty-fifty on the side to win, does that contemplate
   supplies are going from this country in the event of war?
THE PRESIDENT: No, no it does not.
Q What would the odds be then?
THE PRESIDENT: I don't know. I never put the question that way.

Roosevelt had gone on to emphasize that the furnishing of supplies
by the United States did not mean it would be drawn in militarily.
He had summed up by saying: "I think we want to keep out but, on
the other hand, I think we want to do everything we can to keep a
survival of democracy."[35]
    As the year wore on and it became increasingly unlikely that arms
embargo repeal would be accomplished during the present session of
Congress, a new theme began to creep into the President's statements, the idea that repeal would act as a deterrent to the aggressors.
To be sure, that belief was circulating in Washington at the time, and
was reinforced, after the House's unfavorable action on the Bloom
measure at the end of June, by dispatches pouring into the State
Department from U.S. ambassadors in Europe to the effect that
Europeans now felt the dictators would be encouraged to take a
stronger position.[36] Roosevelt himself, citing the dispatches, began
to talk to reporters as he did at a July 4 press conference:

I think you might emphasize a little bit more the fact that the policy of the
Administration is to try to prevent any war in any part of the word. That is the

first policy and anything that can be done to stop a war from starting is a good thing because it does not raise certain questions that would be raised if a war started. That is in words of one syllable.[37]

It is quite unlikey that the President himself, acutely sensing the abnormal ambitions of the "madmen" Hitler and Mussolini, had much faith that the United States could preserve the peace no matter what measures it might take. It would appear that he was now using this new argument in the hope that it might achieve arms embargo repeal. When he asked at the July 4 press conference, "Is it a safe assumption, or would you say that you want the Senate Foreign Relations Committee to go ahead with its consideration of neutrality legislation?" he replied, "Yes, in the interest of preventing war." A week later, however, at another press conference, he revealed that his first thought had not changed at all. Commenting on the vote in the Senate Foreign Relations Committee that very day, putting off consideration of neutrality legislation until the next session of Congress, Roosevelt complained that "if something should happen internationally in the meantime, it would be a pretty difficult thing for Congress to reassemble after the event and pass legislation in the face of an existing war. There is a probability that everybody would be charged with unneutrality at that time."[38]

On the evening of July 18 the administration made one last plea for repeal of the arms embargo at this session of Congress when the President, Secretary Hull, and Vice President John Nance Garner met with Senate leaders of both parties at the White House. Secretary Hull, who all along had been much more convinced than the President that a change in the neutrality law would increase the chances for peace, took this meeting very seriously. Roosevelt, on the other hand, appears to have been convinced that repeal was now hopeless. It was Hull who had persuaded the President to hold the meeting, and Roosevelt, in agreeing to do so, may have been motivated mostly by the thought of its political usefulness for putting his isolationist opponents on record as badly misjudging the threat of war. The administration rested its case for repeal on the possibility of war in Europe by the end of the summer—dispatches to the State Department pointed in that direction, but when Senator Borah informed Hull he had his own private sources of information, more reliable that the State Department's, which indicated there would be no war, the conference collapsed.[39] The President's reaction was described by the two young Washington reporters Alsop and Kintner, who were particularly close to Roosevelt and privy to State Department records and confidential information.[40]

Where Hull seemed almost broken, the President had expected the meeting's conclusion from the start, and was good-humored about it. [He stated] that the Senate must now take the responsibility. Borah put in that there would be "no difficulty about that." Threat the President asked for a pad and pencil, wrote out statements for Hull and Barkley to give the reporters waiting in the White House portico, and said good-bye to his guests. The meeting broke up in laughter.[41]

Roosevelt used this meeting to gain a strong political advantage, coming down heavily in his press conferences in the next few weeks on the responsibility his opponents must take for blocking what was perhaps the last chance to prevent war when they refused to consider repeal of the arms embargo. When asked about repeal, on July 21, Roosevelt answered:

Isn't that closed until January? . . . By action of the Senate? I think that is the best way of handling it. There is no, and there cannot be any, immediate issue before the country because certain groups in the Senate just precluded any action until January, making it perfectly clear, of course—and they have accepted it—that the responsibility rests wholly on them.

Of course, one of the important things to bring out on that—what was it? Tuesday night—is the fact that they were willing to accept the responsibility. And as Steve [Early] told you yesterday, about all we can do between now and January is to pray that there won't be another crisis, and pray awfully hard.

He went on to explain:

For the last three or four years there have been recurring threats. So far they have not eventuated in actual war. Another threat may come without eventuating in actual war. But the United States is not in a position to help in a situation of that kind under the present law—under the embargo—and the members of the Senate, the other night, were fully apprised of that. That was perfectly clearly stated; and several of them accepted the thought that there would be no special session until and unless a world war had actually broken out. In other words, they accepted the responsibility of saying to the Executive Branch of the Government: "There is nothing further you can do to avert war."[42]

In his August 8 press conference he put the blame squarely on the congressional Republicans and about one-fourth of the congressional Democrats. When he was asked, "Mr. President, then the logical second half of the question is this: That the recent Congress also disagreed with you on method, particularly regarding neutrality . . . " he replied:

No, I would not say that, Dick [Harkness]. I would not say they disagreed on methods. What I would say is this: That they made a bet—not the Congress, don't, for Heaven's sake, say, "The Congress," but a substantially unanimous Republican minority in both Houses, both the House and Senate, plus about twenty per cent, twenty-two percent of the House [Democrats] and twenty-five per cent of the Senate [Democrats], have made a bet with the country that the President was wrong. And I hope they win their bet. But, if they do not win their bet, the responsibility is one hundred per cent on a solid Republican minority plus a small minority of the Democrats. . . . . On the neutrality end, they bet the Nation, made a large wager with the Nation, which may affect, if they lose it, about a billion and a half human beings. Now, that is pretty important. They have said: "There will be no war until sufficiently long after we come back. . . . " and I sincerely hope they are right. But, if they are not right and we have another serious international crisis they have tied my hands, and I have practically no power to make an American effort to prevent such a war from breaking out. Now, that is a pretty serious responsibility.

. . . . it is perfectly obvious who will be solely responsible—a solid Republican minority plus twenty to twenty-five per cent of the Democrats. And I hope they win their bet.[43]

In this same press conference, Roosevelt claimed that in making pleas to the dictators he had "averted" war in September 1938 and April 1939. One wonders how much he really believed in the efficacy of his actions at those times. It would seem more likely that he was calling attention to them because he wished to be put on record as a peacekeeper, just as he was attempting to label his opponents ineffective in this regard.

Of course, the administration always had to proceed on the outside chance that there was a possibility of preventing war. Therefore, the administration had engaged in a psychological peace offensive against Hitler in the early part of 1939, "speaking sharply to the little boy and beating him when he sneezes" as Roosevelt had put it, in the terminology of *Alice in Wonderland*.[44] Then, at the time when war was most feared, in April 1939 after Hitler had absorbed Czechoslovakia and Mussolini Albania, Roosevelt, on his own initiative had sprung his "Saturday surprise" April 15 message to the two dictators, asking them to promise they would not attack any of thirty-one nations named, for at least ten years. Hitler's reply was insultingly sarcastic. It is doubtful, however, that the President expected his moral appeal to the dictators to have any long-range deterrent effect, although he might have hoped that it would put off the inevitable a while longer until the western democracies were better prepared.[45] By this time Roosevelt had lost faith in the efficacy of moral appeals, as can be seen in a letter he sent to

Secretary of Agriculture Henry Wallace, only the day before, discouraging Wallace from addressing his own message to the dictators. "The two madmen respect force and force alone," Roosevelt warned.

They will try to disparage the [Wallace] note. There is danger that people in foreign lands and even some in the United States will look on your effort as being in the same category as delivering a sermon to a mad dog. The prestige of your name is so important in world affairs that it should not, in my opinion, be risked at this time. At the present time the most feasible way out is to use methods which would tend to drive a wedge between the two madmen.[46]

Only four days after Roosevelt's message to the dictators, Bullitt expressed to the British ambassador to France Roosevelt's wish that the British adopt conscription.[47] Moral appeals, notwithstanding, the President was still concentrating on preparation. The orientation of his foreign policy during 1939 was toward this goal. If repeal of the arms embargo had been obtained, U.S. preparation in the prewar period would have been complete. Undoubtedly Roosevelt was unhappy with the failure to repeal the embargo before the Second World War began, not because he felt that such action would be a deterrent to Hitler but because it prevented the United States from being ready to make its own contribution to "the survival of democracy," as he had termed it, immediately upon the outbreak of the war. However, shrewd politician that he was, he wove from the defeat a new and more effective position for the administration. He weighted his isolationist opponents with the onus of failing to take steps to try to prevent war, and when next the administration would go to Congress for arms embargo repeal, as he knew it must if the war broke out, it would be in a stronger, less defensive position from which to wage its next battle with the isolationists.

3

PROBLEMS AND SOLUTIONS

When Franklin Roosevelt spoke of "a survival of democracy" in his April 20 dinner meeting with the American Society of Newspaper Editors, he was not idly coining a phrase. He was speaking of a belief and purpose close to his heart throughout the thirties. The way to survival in the early thirties, as he saw it, was to make democracy work at home, to prove to a depression-ridden world that such a form of government could find solutions to economic problems at least as skillfully as the reputedly more efficient dictatorships, and that it could do so without a sacrifice of the political freedoms that the democratic form of government had been established to guarantee and preserve. Conscious of the threat not only to democracy but to the whole value structure of the civilized western world, he became the exemplar, and his voice the explainer, of the democratic way of life to his own people and to peoples abroad. The meaning and purpose of democracy was a constant theme in his radio addresses. Unswerving faith in its revival and growth was a significant factor in his own leadership. The perceptive American journalist Karl von Wiegand understood this well when he wrote, "Roosevelt is Hitler's most dangerous opponent. Roosevelt fights for his democratic aims with the same fanatic idealism as does the Fuehrer for national socialism."[1]

In the beginning, one of his purposes as President was to unite the various sections of the country, to forge common bonds among the many disparate elements of the population.[2] By the time of the

1936 presidential campaign, however, opponents were accusing him of fomenting class hatred by making special appeals to workers while castigating "organized money" as "the forces of selfishness and lust for power."[3] But again, as the thirties wore on and the threat from dictatorships grew apace, Roosevelt began to stress that a special kind of unity was needed to face effectively threats from abroad. He concluded a radio address to the *New York Herald-Tribune* Forum in October 1938 with the following plea:

Let us work with greater unity for peace among the nations of the world, for restraint, for negotiations and for community of effort. Let us work for the same ideals within our own borders in our relations with each other, so that we may, if the test ever comes, have that unity of will with which alone a democracy can successfully meet its enemies.[4]

Conditions at the start of 1939 dictated that the annual message that year dwell at length on foreign affairs. Significantly, a good part of the speech developed the theme of unity. "A strong and united nation may be destroyed if it is unprepared against sudden attack," the President declared.

But even a nation well armed and well organized from a strictly military standpoint may, after a period of time, meet defeat if it is unnerved by self-distrust, endangered by class prejudice, by dissension between capital and labor, by false economy and by other unsolved social problems at home.

In meeting the troubles of the world we must meet them as one people—with a unity born of the fact that for generations those who have come to our shores, representing many kindreds and tongues, have been welded by common opportunity into a united patriotism. If another form of government can present a united front in its attack on a democracy, the attack must and will be met by a united democracy. Such a democracy can and must exist in the United States.[5]

When Roosevelt referred to "class prejudice" in that message he was thinking of something quite different from antagonisms toward the rentier class that he himself had been accused of inspiring. He was acutely aware of prejudice from the other direction, of the hostility of the "haves" toward the "have-nots," and of the clear differentiation and segregation of immigrant groups in America.[6] The New Deal had been dedicated to bringing minorities into the mainstream of American life and in this sense had always tried to foster a greater unity in the country. Now in the turbulent climate of 1939 Roosevelt himself was consciously avoiding provocative statements in both the domestic and foreign policy spheres, and by so doing was, if not welding the American people together, at least preventing them from flying farther apart.

At the same time, consummate statesman and politician that he was, he gave careful attention to the creation of a psychology of international good will as well. Thus the United States' "special relationship" with Great Britain, persisting to our day, had its beginning at this time.

The closeness of Roosevelt and Churchill and the postwar solidarity of the two nations makes it difficult to remember a time when the "special relationship" did not exist. Yet a coming together of this nature was not initially a part of Roosevelt's policy, but only developed as international conditions worsened during his second administration. Roosevelt, harboring a certain mistrust of British foreign policy in the early thirties, had stated it on more than one occasion.[7] To his ambassador to Britain, Robert Bingham, he had written in 1935:

Many years ago I came to the reluctant conclusion that it is a mistake to make advances to the British Government; practical results can be accomplished only when they make the advances themselves. They are a funny people and, though always polite, can be counted on when things are going well with them to show a national selfishness towards other nations which makes mutual helpfulness very difficult to accomplish. Their average conception of mutuality differs from mine.[8]

Particularly suspicious of the British Tories, Roosevelt, even in the last months of the thirties, was still voicing doubts. The chairman of the Democratic National Committee, Jim Farley, reported that just after the outbreak of the Second World War the President confided to him:

The trouble with the British is that they have for several hundred years been controlled by the upper classes. The upper classes control all trade and commerce; therefore the policy of the British government relates entirely to the protection of this class.

And, Farley went on to elaborate:

The President was never very generous before me in his reference to the British in the prewar days. He was forever expressing doubt that Britain would ever go through for anyone else, declaring they were for England and England alone all the time. However, he always had the highest admiration and respect for Winston Churchill.[9]

No doubt Roosevelt, disenchanted with Chamberlain, looked forward to a possible infusion of new blood into the British ruling circles. It was perhaps in anticipation of such a change and of the coming importance of Churchill in England that he advised Farley in the summer of 1939, just prior to Farley's scheduled European tour: "Be my eyes and ears on the trip, Jim, and pick up as much information as you can for me. See as many people as you can. See Winston Churchill. See Chamberlain or anybody in his Cabinet." Five years later Farley remarked to Lord Beaverbrook, "In 1939 Roosevelt told me he [Churchill] was the one man in England I should meet."[10]

It would be another two years before Roosevelt himself would meet Churchill, but in 1939 he began the process of forming close personal relationships with English dignitaries when the reigning sovereign of Britain, for the first time in history, paid a visit to the United States. This visit had been conceived as early as the summer of 1937 when Roosevelt's envoy to King George VI's coronation had suggested that if the King planned to visit Canada, as the Canadian Prime Minister, Mackenzie King, was trying to persuade him to do, he ought to pay a visit to the United States as well. The King was receptive to this idea, and a visit to both countries was subsequently arranged for the summer of 1939.[11] The official biographer of King George VI, John Wheeler-Bennett, later attached much importance to this visit, crediting Roosevelt with a well-executed step in diplomacy. Wheeler-Bennett wrote:

In his original conception of the visit of the King and Queen, President Roosevelt had had the international situation very prominently in mind, and with greater far-sightedness than many of his countrymen. Just as the presence of Their Majesties in Canada had presented to the world an irrefutable demonstration of Commonwealth solidarity, so, he hoped, would their visit to the United States offer a similar proof of Anglo-American friendship.[12]

Eleanor Roosevelt felt that it was primarily American public opinion that the President had in mind when he invited George VI to visit the United States.

My husband invited them to Washington largely because, believing that we all might soon be engaged in a life and death struggle, in which Great Britain would be our first line of defense, he hoped that the visit would create a bond of friendship between the people of the two countries. He knew that, though there is always in this country a certain amount of criticism and superficial ill-feeling toward the British, in time of danger something deeper comes to the surface, and the British and we stand firmly together, with confidence in our common heritage and ideas. The visit of the king and queen, he hoped, would be a reminder of this deep bond. In many ways it proved even more successful than he had expected.[13]

At that time, Roosevelt openly expressed to King George VI his concern that the forthcoming visit have the right effect on American public opinion. "I know you will not mind my telling you," he wrote to the King in November 1938,

that in my judgment, to the American people, the essential democracy of yourself and the Queen makes the greatest appeal of all. . . . If you could stay with us at Hyde Park for two or three days, the simplicity and naturalness of such a visit would produce a most excellent effect——

In all, Their Majesties spent four days in the United States, ending their stay with a most significant twenty-four hours at Hyde Park. Roosevelt, obviously thrilled that the whole trip had lived up to his expectations, wrote afterward to his English cousin, Arthur Murray:

I cannot write you of the many delightful events in the visit of the King and Queen, but I can tell you that it was a tremendous success. They came to a friendly but curious American public and four days later they left an impression of real understanding and affection behind them. The most appealing scene of all was at the Hyde Park station at eleven o'clock the night they left. All the neighborhood of village and country people—five thousand of them—to say goodbye, and as the train pulled out the King and Queen had tears in their eyes and wholly unexpectedly the crowd sang "Auld Lang Syne" and "He's a Jolly Good Fellow." The whole trip did an immense amount of good, and, incidentally, I formed a really deep and affectionate regard for your Sovereign.[14]

Roosevelt's last statement hints of an unexpected bonus derived from the visit. The King's biographer confirmed that the President discovered, to his surprise, that the King and Queen were more than just the "two nice young people" he had expected to meet, and that he could engage the King in discussions on an advanced level. During the interlude at Hyde Park Roosevelt took the King aside for long sessions covering a fairly full spectrum of international and domestic problems. The President broached strategic problems, even speaking of securing bases for the United States in the Caribbean, a full year before the destroyers-for-bases swap was conceived. In a memorandum of June 12, made the morning after a late-night conversation at Hyde Park, George VI recorded, under a section labeled "F.D.R.'s ideas in case of War":

Trinidad Patrol. Base for his fleet at Trinidad to fuel and replenish stores. From this base he can patrol the Atlantic with ships & aeroplanes on a radius of approximately 1000 miles on a sector of latitude of Haiti to latitude of Brazil. This patrol should locate any enemy fleet which tried to ger to S. Am. or the West Indies.

Bermuda Patrol. Base as above. To patrol N. Atlantic from Cape Cod to Florida, with ships and aeroplanes to prevent submarines from attacking convoys.

Brazil. Germans have an air base at Natal Cape St. Roque also a landing ground on the island of Fernando Noronha 200 miles from the coast. Brazil is pretty sure to kick out the Germans. He would then use it himself.

Haiti, Cuba, & West Indies are potential friendly bases.

The idea is that U.S.A. should relieve us of these responsibilities, but can it be done without a declaration of war?[15]

It was as early as 1936 that Roosevelt, primarily interested in protection of the American continent, first conceived plans for bases on a wide ring from Newfoundland to the Caribbean islands.[16] Now he explored this and other considerations with the King, at a time when both men felt "they were approaching the point at which one no longer said 'if' war should come, but 'when' war should come."[17] In this spirit they tackled their individual and joint problems. A reference to the Neutrality Act in the King's notes, for instance, comes in such a way as to indicate that Roosevelt was considering repeal not as a peace effort but as a means to assist England when war came. "On mentioning the Neutrality Act," George VI recorded, "the President gave us hopes that something could be done to make it less difficult for the U.S.A. to help us."[18]

In the course of their talks Roosevelt allowed the King such insights into the general processes of his thought that George VI was certain from this time forward that he understood Roosevelt very well. As will be seen, the King came away with special insights into Roosevelt's attitude and tactics in regard to American public opinion. As Harry Hopkins, Roosevelt's emissary to England in 1941, later recorded:

The King on his part told me how greatly he appreciated the President's speeches and said he was sure from the last visit that he knew what was deeply embedded in the President's mind.[19]

On the first day of September 1939, Hitler moved into Poland. In response, Britain and France declared war on Germany on September 3. The Second World War had begun, and repeal of the arms embargo now became essential. In one way it might appear that the administration's task had been made easier, for the unalterable fact of war itself was coupled with the American public's predominant sympathy for England and France. This sympathy was so pronounced that Roosevelt could say to the country, in his fireside chat on the evening of September 3: "This nation will remain a neutral nation, but I cannot ask that every American remain neutral in thought as well."[20] On the other hand, fear of being drawn into the war was bound to be a counter consideration on the part of the public and would be the theme emphasized by the isolationists in their campaign against repeal.

Roosevelt approached the issue with caution, delaying the call for a special session of Congress until soundings were made on the Hill and the administration received favorable reports, predicting approximately sixty senatorial votes in its behalf.[21] The political considerations were, as usual, uppermost in FDR's mind, and White House files on the subject of "neutrality" reveal something of the nitty-gritty problems that impelled what the President characterized as his "walking-on-eggs" attitude until the all-important new bill had passed. A memorandum on Republican strategy, for instance, marked for filing as "personal and private," reads as follows:

Re: Neutrality Act

From very reliable sources. As of today the plans of the Republican National Committee Publicity Section (Waltman) in respect of the Neutrality Act are as follows:

(1) A period of resistance to repeal designed to disseminate the impression that the President will, if not restrained, get the country into war. This will be accomplished by a "filibuster" by present outspoken foes of modification of the Act–Borah, Nye, Vandenberg, etc.–to create an uneasiness that the President's intentions or "blundering" under his "vague" powers are dangerously likely to get the country into war.

(2) This period will last up to the point where the benefit [,] or political damage to the President will be outweighed by the political damage to the Republican Party from pro-allied and business profits sentiment.

(3) At that point the Republican direction will be taken up by men like Martin and McNary, who will then say that all the Republicans are really objecting to is vague personal powers of the President and that if the President really means what he says about national unity and a cessation of politics and will sit down with Republican leaders to draft a new bill which will be called "An Act to Protect the United States Against Involvement in War," the Republican leaders are sure that a satisfactory bill can be worked out. Then they will cooperate in drafting a bill which in substance meets the needs of the Allies and the demands of business men. But they will then publicize the act as a "victory for peace" for which the credit goes to the Republicans by reason of the fact that the new bill curtails the "vague and broad" powers which the President has asked for himself.[22]

Although the memorandum is not an adequate forecast in every detail it does indicate the general political framework within which

Roosevelt had to work. As in the springtime of that year, when the arms embargo repeal had first been considered in Congress, the opposition was to make a powerful argument on the question of granting the President too much discretionary power, the inference being that if the present neutrality legislation remained unchanged the Congress, rather than the President, would be more in control and less likely to bring the country to war. On the other hand, Roosevelt might have been encouraged by the assumption that the minority leaders, Martin and McNary, did not intend to be personally obstructive.

On his own part, Roosevelt, as soon as the war broke out and with Wilson's error uppermost in his mind,[23] made attempts to foster a bipartisanship in foreign policy. When announcing the special session of Congress in a telegram of September 13 to majority and minority House and Senate leaders, he added the request that they come to the capital a day before the session "for an informal conference with me."[24] Alfred M. Landon and Colonel Frank Knox, who had been the Republican presidential and vice-presidential candidates in 1936 but who were also so much in tune with Roosevelt's foreign policy that they were being called upon to speak and write on behalf of repeal,[25] were also invited. Alsop and Kintner reveal, however, that the meeting did not deal with "fundamental questions of foreign policy," because the President and Secretary Hull remembered the consequences of Roosevelt's unusually frank remarks to the Senate Military Affairs Committee the preceding February. "Most of the men invited arrived in expectation of portentous revelations," write Alsop and Kintner. But, "when the Republicans found that they had been invited to a conference on legislative strategy, they grew somewhat restive. The House leader, Joe Martin, whispered to Landon at one point, 'I'd like to know what we're here for,' and both Landon and Colonel Knox were annoyed at having been asked to travel so far to act as mere window-dressing." Nevertheless, Republican leaders in Congress did announce afterward that they would not make a partisan issue out of the repeal measure.[26]

For carrying out its "legislative strategy" the administration also enlisted the aid of private citizens. Roosevelt gratefully accepted the offers of two prominent businessmen, Thomas W. Lamont, a J.P. Morgan partner, and Myron C. Taylor, a former chairman of the board of United States Steel, to work at winning the necessary congressional votes. Lamont was to become a strong supporter of Roosevelt's foreign policy, continuing both to offer advice and to work actively for the administration. How very closely the administration worked with these interested volunteers can be seen in the nature and tone of the correspondence with them. For example, a letter from Steve Early to Myron Taylor on congressional voting patterns reads as follows:

We have reason to believe that the accompanying record of the vote taken by the Senate committee on foreign relations is correct. The vote, of course, refers to the rejection by the committee [in July] on a vote of 12 to 11 of the proposal for the Senate to take up the revision of the Neutrality Act for consideration before the Congress adjourned.

This question, consequently, never came before the Senate for a vote but I expect to be able to give you within a day or·so information concerning the attitude of various senators on the question of revision of the neutrality laws.[27]

In addition to trying to cut down Republican opposition, the administration had to be even more concerned about defecting Democrats, for they had made the difference in the spring defeat of neutrality revision. In the House, 61 Democrats had voted in favor of the Vorys amendment. Although only 17 of these votes had come from the South, that was a considerable number to lose from the section that was the most interventionist-minded in the country. Conservative anti-Roosevelt southerners were a formidable problem in both houses. Adopting a kind of southern strategy that was a counterpart to his effort at bipartisanship, Roosevelt now attempted to win back the southern contingent by asking Senators Tom Connally of Texas and James Byrnes of South Carolina to play a large role in getting neutrality repeal through the Senate.[28]

In his address of September 21, opening the special session of Congress, Roosevelt struck essentially two themes. He made a plea for nonpartisanship and he said that the administration's purpose in asking for neutrality law revision was to keep America out of the war. "I give to you my deep and unalterable conviction," he declared,

based on years of experience as a worker in the field of international peace, that by repeal of the embargo the United States will more probably remain at peace than if the law remains as it stands today. I say this because with the repeal of the embargo, this Government clearly and definitely will insist that American citizens and American ships keep away from the immediate perils of the actual zones of conflict.[29]

The design was to replace the arms embargo with a cash-and-carry stipulation for all exports to belligerents, and the new neutrality act was also to include a provision for keeping American ships out of waters that the President might designate as combat zones. Roosevelt favored such substitutions and additions as a means of avoiding "incidents" on the high seas.[30]

The address made no mention of the administration's basic reason for wanting repeal of the arms embargo—its desire to aid Britain and France. As Hull explained in his *Memoirs*, the administration could not openly state this desire, for "with isolationism still powerful and militant in the United States, it would have been the peak of folly to make aid to the democracies an issue in connection with neutrality legislation." Had Roosevelt been able to be candid on this score, however, an alignment with the democracies could justifiably have been presented as a means of keeping this nation at peace. Hull also recalled that he and the President "were sincere in our belief that the new legislation would afford us a better chance of keeping out of the war than the old legislation because, if Britain and France won the war, we could remain at peace, whereas if Germany won there was every likelihood that we should soon have to fight."[31] Roosevelt, in his press conference with the American Society of Newspaper Editors on April 20, had given every indication that he shared this view.

Although the administration's strategy was to keep debate to a minimum in order to speed the arms embargo repeal through the Congress as quickly as possible,[32] the isolationists were not easily put off. In a well-organized movement they took to the airwaves, starting their campaign with a radio address by the leader of the Senate isolationists, Senator Borah, on September 14, in which he contended that the administration in truth desired to aid Britain and France and that once the United States started selling them arms it would be on its way to intervention in their war. Borah's speech was followed by radio appeals from other prominent men, including Charles A. Lindbergh, Norman Thomas, and Herbert Hoover.[33]

The isolationists' campaign was effective. Mail began to flood congressional offices, with the overwhelming proportion of the messages in support of the arms embargo.[34] Roosevelt's original optimism turned to apprehension. On September 11 he had written: "My own personal opinion is that we can get the votes in the House and the Senate but that the principal difficulty will be to prevent a filibuster in the latter."[35] But on a September 19 telegram to the President from a Boston attorney, Conrad W. Crooker, offering his assistance, the following White House notation was made: "S.T.E. & General Watson to handle   We want all the help we can get".[36]

Now Roosevelt began to work quietly to counter the isolationist assault upon public opinion. New York's Clark Eichelberger, long active in American internationalist organizations, had earlier offered his services. The President now accepted his help. Eichelberger planned to form a new committee, the Non-Partisan Committee for Peace through Revision of the Neutrality Act. Following a suggestion from Hull, he prevailed upon William Allen White, the venerable Republican editor of the *Emporia* (Kansas) *Gazette,* to head it. White was the outstandingly logical choice. He was Roosevelt's friend—in the 1936 campaign FDR himself had defined his relationship with William Allen White when he told an Emporia crowd: "Bill White is with me three and a half years out of every four."[37] He was also considered *the* spokesman of middle-class America.[38] The White Committee, as it came to be called, did strenuous and effective work throughout October at the grass-roots level through its many local chapters and through sponsorship of radio addresses by prominent citizens. In other ways, Roosevelt himself worked behind the scenes. He enlisted support from such friendly opinion leaders as Cardinal Mundelein of Chicago—leaders who represented or could influence groups potentially hostile to repeal of the arms embargo, such as Irish Catholics, the American Legion, and labor groups.[39]

The administration, now aided by the work of its friends and perhaps also by the isolationists' failure to find enough financial backing, began to regain its confidence. However, periods of optimism continued to fluctuate with moods of concern. By mid-October it was the House rather than the Senate that was causing the most worry.[40] In the spring the administration had been more wary of the Senate and more confident of success in the House. The vote on the Vorys amendment had been a rude shock, however, and now there continued to be concern about the unpredictability of the House. In an October 16 letter the ever zealous Ickes alerted the President to possible trouble:

Congressman Dempsey of New Mexico called me this morning. He talked with the Speaker on Saturday and asked him whether a check had been made on the neutrality legislation. The Speaker's reply was that those had been checked who had voted against the Administration's neutrality position at the regular session. Dempsey then asked whether those who had voted "right" at the last session had been checked. The Speaker's answer to this was "No, that is not necessary". Then Dempsey remarked that it was necessary because they were just as likely to change their position as those who had voted "wrong". He named three such persons to the Speaker's great surprise. The Speaker then said that he would have a check made. Dempsey thinks that it is very important to assure that those who voted with the Administration at the regular session are still with it.[41]

Eventually, and in spite of alarms toward the end, the arms embargo repeal passed both the House and the Senate by comfortable margins—63 to 30 in the Senate and 243 to 181 in the House. On November 4 Roosevelt happily signed the Neutrality Act of 1939. As a section the South had contributed the most votes in both houses, registering for repeal by the lopsided margins of 23 to 2 in the Senate and 110 to 8 in the House. The Midwest had recorded the strongest opposition. Although there was some crossing of party lines, the voting in both houses was heavily partisan in nature.[42]

By a strategy of effective behind-the-scenes action, of close cooperation with interested private citizens and citizens' organizations, and of subdued rhetoric, Roosevelt had won the day. He had been careful to avoid any actions, as well as words, which might have added grist to the isolationist mill. Asking Lord Tweedsmuir, Governor General of Canada, to postpone his visit to the United States until arms embargo repeal was accomplished, Roosevelt explained: "As you have probably sensed, I am almost literally walking on eggs and, having delivered my message to the Congress, and having good prospects of the bill going through, I am at the moment saying nothing, seeing nothing and hearing nothing." He also put restraints upon the more exuberant members of his cabinet. Ickes, concerned about the danger of the European war splintering the various national groups in the United States, wanted to accept an invitation to address a Polish gathering in Chicago. Roosevelt wrote him, however: "You are right about leading the right kind of public opinion in this country. As a matter of practical politics I think it is better for us to withhold any speeches, such as talks to Poles, etc., for just a very short time, i.e., until we get the embargo repeal through. In other words, merely a matter of timing."[43]

By the end of 1939, without exciting the American people, Roosevelt had faced and effectively solved the most pressing problems facing the country that year. He had drawn closer to England diplomatically and had put his country in a position to give practical assistance to the Allies. His real desire in asking for repeal of the arms embargo—to aid Britain and France—was surmised by practically all representatives of the media.[44] Indeed, he was not exactly trying to cloak the real feelings of the government, since he had asked in his fireside chat of September 3 that this nation not "remain neutral in thought." Yet both the President and his advisers had felt it necessary to present arms embargo repeal as a means to insure United States neutrality, undoubtedly because they had gauged public opinion to be such that only in this way could the repeal issue have been resolved successfully.

It was a time of great uncertainty in the public mind. Public opinion polls, which seldom influence congressmen[45] but which the President had a great respect for,[46] had shown much variation during the year. In the spring, majority sentiment had favored repeal of the arms embargo, but by August a Gallup poll showed 57 percent approving the recent congressional defeat of neutrality law revision. As World War II broke there was an even division on the question: "If Congress does meet in special session should it change the present Neutrality Law so that the U.S. could sell war materials to England and France?" Then, in September and October, majority sentiment again began to register in favor of arms embargo repeal.[47]

In this unsteady climate, and with fear of American involvement in the war uppermost in the public mind, the administration could not have afforded complete candor. The able career diplomat Jay Pierrepont Moffat, chief of the Division of European Affairs in the State Department, recorded in his Diary entry for September 19, 1939: "If the vote were to be held today the Administration would win hands down, but the opposition by labeling itself the 'Peace Party' is rolling up considerable strength. The battle can [not] be won unless false tactics are used." Subsequent polls tend to bear out this assessment by Moffat and to justify the administration strategy approved by the President. In a Gallup poll released on November 8, 62 percent answered yes to the question: "Do you approve the change which Congress made in the Neutrality Act which permits nations at war to buy arms and airplanes in this country?" The breakdowns, however, give the more revealing information. In two polls taken in October, while 56 percent at that time said they wanted repeal of the arms embargo, when this number was asked "why" from 31 to 34 percent chose, as the "main reason," the response "to improve business in this country," 26 to 31 percent answered "to keep the United States out of war," and only 20 to 23 percent said they were motivated chiefly by the desire "to help England and France."[48]

4

A QUESTION OF SURVIVAL

When war began in Europe Americans wished the Allies well but fervently hoped they would not be called upon to participate again militarily. In polls taken in the early months of the war a majority went on record against intervention, even if it appeared that France and England would be defeated.[1] In the winter of 1939-1940 a kind of Pollyannaish attitude gripped this nation, which, understandably enough, balked at the prospect of engaging in another world war only twenty years after the Great War of 1917-1918. Roosevelt, apprehensive about the condition of the American mind and possibly anticipating a need to call once more upon William Allen White to help with American public opinion, wrote a revealing letter to White on December 14, 1939. The letter covers so many facets of Roosevelt's thinking on a wide range of international and domestic issues that it deserves to be quoted at length.

Dear Bill: I have had a fairly quiet few weeks with a chance for more thought than during the neutrality bill period and I have been gradually getting to the point where I need a few helpful thoughts from the philosopher of Emporia. That is why I hope that the next time you come East you will come and spend the night at the White House and let me sit you on the sofa after supper and talk over small matters like the world problems.

Here is the thought for you to devote thought to. Taking things in their broadest aspect, the world situation seems to me to be getting rather progressively worse as the weeks go by. No human being, with the best of information, has the slightest idea how this war is going to come out. But, the

54

fact remains that there are four or five possibilities, each leading either to greater chaos or to the kind of truce which could last for only a very short period.

As you know, I do not entertain the thought of some of the statesmen of 1918 that the world can make, or we can help the world to achieve, a permanently lasting peace—that is a peace which we would visualize as enduring for a century or more. On the other hand, I do not want this country to take part in a patched up temporizing peace which would blow up in our faces in a year or two.

. . .

If . . . Germany and Russia win the war or force a peace favorable to them, the situation of your civilization and mine is indeed in peril. Our world trade would be at the mercy of the combine and our increasingly better relations with our twenty neighbors to the south would end—unless we were willing to go to war in their behalf against a German-Russian dominated Europe.

What worries me, especially, is that public opinion over here is patting itself on the back every morning and thanking God for the Atlantic Ocean (and the Pacific Ocean). We greatly underestimate the serious implications to our own future and I fear most people are merely going around saying:

"Thank God for Roosevelt and Hull—no matter what happens, they will keep us out of war. We have enormous confidence in their ability to handle our international relations."

The Lord and you know perfectly well that Roosevelt and Hull fully expect to keep us out of war—but, on the other hand, we are not going around thanking God for allowing us physical safety within our continental limits.

Things move with such terrific speed, these days, that it really is essential to us to think in broader terms and, in effect, to warn the American people that they, too, should think of possible ultimate results in Europe and the Far East.

Therefore, my sage old friend, my problem is to get the American people to think of conceivable consequences without scaring the American people into thinking that they are going to be dragged into this war.[2]

During the first winter's lull in fighting, Roosevelt himself was making mental preparations for future contingencies, and, as his letter to White indicates, the task of "get[ting] the American people to think of conceivable consequences" was very much on his mind. Undoubtedly, with this long and flattering letter, he was preparing the way should the need arise to approach White once more with a request for assistance. He also readily accepted offers which might come from other private citizens to help with public opinion. In November, the White House had okayed the suggestion of Conrad W. Crooker—the organizer of the Non-Partisan Neutrality Committee of New England, which had helped in the repeal of the arms embargo —to continue, in Crooker's words, an "organized effort . . . non partisan in character, and intended to emphasixe [*sic*] not only our neutrality, but the great and ever continuing need of adequate preparedness."[3]

In the respite period before the outbreak of Hitler's expected spring campaign in the West, Roosevelt made a sudden and startling dramatic gesture which led to questioning then, and since, as to the thought and purpose behind the act. He sent his long-time friend and personal confidant, Undersecretary of State Sumner Welles, on a mission to the four major European capitals, Rome, Berlin, Paris, and London, in that order, in the months of February and March 1940. Although Welles has reported that he and Roosevelt had been discussing the possibility of such a trip for some time,[4] it would appear that the actual decision to go through with it was made by the President alone and quite suddenly. The highly respected journalist Raymond Clapper, present at an off-the-record discussion on the night of February 12, 1940 between correspondents and Assistant Secretary of State Messersmith at the home of Eugene Meyer, publisher of the *Washington Post,* recorded in his notes: "Welles trip primarily Roosevelt's idea and developed suddenly. Messersmith reluctant to discuss it beyond that."[5]

In deciding to send Welles as his emissary to Europe Roosevelt appears to have been thinking that the trip might yield desirable results in more than one respect. Ideally, the mission might prove a step in the direction of peace, and indeed it would appear that Roosevelt felt a try had to be made before the inevitable spring offensive got underway. However, he was hardly optimistic on that score. In Welles's words, Roosevelt "admitted frankly that the chances seemed to him about one in a thousand that anything at all could be done to change the course of events. On the other hand, he felt that no possibility, however remote and however improbable, should be overlooked. He believed that his obligations to the American people made it imperative for him to leave no stone unturned."[6] The war had made Roosevelt rather desperately concerned with the question of peace, for it must have been quite evident to him that the longer the war continued the greater would be the chances for American involvement. Therefore it is not surprising to find Alsop and Kintner writing:"It is nevertheless true that since the war the President had placed an increasing emphasis on peace-making, which was not necessarily a part of his previous plans."[7] The Welles mission, with "no proposals to offer and no commitments whatever to put forward on the part of the United States,"[8] was to sound out the chances for an effective peace.

There were other purposes, equally important, attached to the mission. If just and lasting peace seemed a rather fleeting prize, at least Welles's probing might be helpful in gathering information. A sophisticated and experienced diplomat, he was to undertake for the President, from his top-level vantage point, a first-class job of reporting. Roosevelt was unsure of the informational feedback he was getting from the key capitals. Welles was to do what Roosevelt was accustomed to asking of other emissaries, to be his "eyes and ears," and to come back with clarifying impressions of the various leaders, especially the Nazis. Welles would have the added advantage, over American ambassadors in the European capitals, of traveling from one capital to another and of being able to use information gathered in one place in the next capital to which he was going.[9]

For Welles, the trip appears to have had a third purpose. There has been some speculation that he was seriously considering the possibility of forming a strong bloc among the neutrals.[10] In back of his mind he seems more than Roosevelt to have entertained the possibility of reaching a kind of modus vivendi with Germany. However, he received such insulting treatment at the hands of the German leaders, Foreign Minister von Ribbentrop in particular, that he returned icily contemptuous of the Nazis, declaring his conviction that there could be no way of finding a cordial existence with the barbaric leaders of the Third Reich.[11]

Soon after Welles's return, the anticipated spring offensive began. The Allies had expected the attack to come in northern France, but on April 9 Hitler surprised the world by beginning his western assault in Norway and Denmark. Denmark was taken in a matter of hours, and Norway was overrun in a few weeks. It was at the time of the Norwegian invasion that Roosevelt became convinced that America would eventually have to enter the war.[12] This is not to say, as the Beardian-type revisionists who belong to the conspiracy school of American history see it, that there was ever deliberate planning on the part of the President to involve the United States in a global war. Roosevelt simply continued, as he had been doing all along, to take whatever opportunities were open to him to aid the western democracies. Although he now clearly discerned the inevitable entry, in the nature of things there was no overall master scheme to bring this about, nor could there be, given the ambivalence within which a democratic leader, responsible at the bar of public opinion, must operate in the foreign policy arena. In the months to come one sees again and again simply the familiar pattern of reaction to the necessities of each separate crisis.

Continuing the blitzkrieg in the West, on May 10 Hitler invaded

the neutral countries of Belgium and the Netherlands. Holland fell in
five days, Belgium capitulated on May 28, and by June 4 the British
expeditionary force had been driven off the continent. An aroused
American public, stunned by the realities of blitzkreig warfare,
looked to the President for both action and reassurance, while the
more internationalist segment of the public clamored for a strong
stand by our government. On May 16 Roosevelt addressed the
Congress on the subject of national defense, on May 26 he spoke to
the nation directly, and on May 31 he sent a request to Congress for
additional appropriations for defense. Although some citizens complained that his graphic descriptions of air distances in the May 16
speech were frightening, others felt that he was not going far enough
at this critical time.[13]

The May 16 message contained the now famous phrase, "I should
like to see this nation geared up to the ability to turn out at least
50,000 planes a year." When stressing national defense, Roosevelt
intimated that the war indeed might be coming closer to these
shores. "Our objective is still peace," he reiterated,

peace at home and peace abroad. Nevertheless, we stand ready not only to spend
millions for defense but to give our service and even our lives for the
maintenance of our American liberties.[14]

Entering now the eighteen-month period preceding Pearl Harbor,
which has come to be known in the history of those years as the
"defense period," Roosevelt set up in this month of May a new
coordinating committee to supervise industrial mobilization and
national preparation for "defense." This was the second time in less
than a year that a committee of this nature had been created, but
now Roosevelt was more committed, given the present state of
public opinion, to taking such a step. There had been an earlier
effort, less intense as far as FDR was concerned, with the creation of
the War Resources Board the previous August. That development
had come about through the urging of Assistant Secretary of War
Louis Johnson, who had finally persuaded Roosevelt to appoint an
advisory board of industrial leaders charged with reviewing the War
Department's Industrial Mobilization Plan. Since the War Resources
Board was chaired by Stettinius, New Dealers had suspected that it
represented the J.P. Morgan interests, and they had objected to the
fact that there was no counterbalancing representation from labor
organizations. For various reasons Roosevelt had had the board's
report, completed in October 1939, suppressed. His own explan-

ation, in a letter to Frank Knox, read as follows:

Have you noticed that, as you suggested in your letter, I have been trying to kill all war talk? I have treated the report of the War Resources Committee as just an ordinary instance of normal preparedness work and they will go home in two weeks with my blessing.[15]

Now, in his May 28 press conference FDR disclosed that he was reviving, under authority from an old 1916 statute, the Advisory Commission to the Council of National Defense. Under the provisions of the 1916 act the Council of National Defense was a body composed of six cabinet members and the Advisory Commission was to have not more than seven people, representing the various economic specialties. As Roosevelt set up his National Defense Advisory Commission, however, it was to report directly to the President. Thus the intermediary of the Defense Council (cabinet members) was in effect eliminated, and the National Defense Advisory Commission (often abbreviated as the NDAC) would have an existence of its own, outside of any agency, and a direct relationship with the President.

The members of the NDAC were as follows:

> for Industrial Production, William S. Knudsen, President of General Motors;
>
> for Industrial Materials, Edward R. Stettinius, Chairman of the Board of U.S. Steel;
>
> for Labor, Sidney Hillman, President of the Amalgamated Clothing Workers of America;
>
> for Price Stabilization, Leon Henderson of the SEC;
>
> for Transportation, Ralph Budd, Director of the American Railway Engineering Association and Chairman of the Burlington;
>
> for Farm Products, Chester C. Davis, on the Board of Governors of the Federal Reserve System;
>
> for Consumer Protection, Dr. Harriet Elliott, Dean of Women at the University of North Carolina;
>
> and the Secretary to the Commission, William H. McReynolds, a career civil servant.

The fact that labor and consumers were represented on the commission took care of previous objections in New Deal circles to the War Resources Board. Roosevelt's own wish to keep mobilization in his own hands was also protected by the structure of the NDAC, for it was to have no chairman and thus no one man who would now be in a position comparable to Bernard Baruch, who during World War I had literally run the economy from his vantage point as chairman of the War Industries Board.

There has been much speculation about Roosevelt's reasons for not wanting to create a czar to supervise defense mobilization. There is good reason to believe (his speeches at the time include this theme) that he was opposed to sacrificing any of the wages and hours gains under the New Deal, which might very well happen if an industrialist were given extensive powers to run the economy. Most likely Roosevelt was motivated, above all, by jealousy of his own prerogative. However, if he kept controls in his own hand, he would then be in a better position to also protect the social gains of the New Deal. His own explanation, to the Business Advisory Council of the Department of Commerce on May 23, 1940, was as follows: "I am not going to set up a War Industries Board and turn a billion dollar or two billion dollar program over to five complete outsiders who don't know anything about running government. It would be unconstitutional; the final responsibility is mine and I can't delegate it."[16]

The NDAC was created to speed war production. Therefore, Knudsen and Stettinius, in charge of Industrial Production and Industrial Materials, respectively, were given full-time appointments, while the members of the commission not directly concerned with industrial production were to serve part-time, gathering statistics and readying themselves for activity in the future if necessary.[17] There was an imperative need for expansion in the war industries, for, as Roosevelt himself later defined the situation, "although prior to June, 1940, a limited amount of military equipment had been purchased by the British and the French, there was comparatively very little armament production in American plants."[18]

Roosevelt's "defense" program was in a very real sense one of defense at a distance. He did not dissimulate with the American people on this score. With the fall of France imminent, Roosevelt in a speech at Charlottesville, Virginia, on June 10 committed the nation to all-out aid to Britain. The most significant part of that address, which may be ranked as Roosevelt's most important speech in the two-year period before Pearl Harbor, is the following passage:

In our American unity, we will pursue two obvious and simultaneous courses; we will extend to the opponents of force the material resources of this nation; and, at the same time, we will harness and speed up the use of those resources in order that we ourselves in the Americas may have equipment and training equal to the task of any emergency and every defense.[19]

In his first important speech after the spring blitzkrieg, Roosevelt had hinted at such a move, when he said to Congress on May 16:

For the permanent record, I ask the Congress not to take any action which would in any way hamper or delay the delivery of American-made planes to foreign nations which have ordered them, or seek to purchase new planes. That, from the point of view of our own national defense, would be extremely short-sighted.[20]

The inference was that the western democracies were indeed our own first line of defense, but at Charlottesville Roosevelt was no longer "asking" that Congress recognize this; he was declaring, "we *will* [emphasis mine] extend to the opponents of force the material resources of this nation." Winston Churchill had been asking Roosevelt to declare nonbelligerency for the United States and at least one diplomatic historian feels that the President began that process at Charlottesville.[21]

It is the feeling of Roosevelt's daughter, Anna, that the Charlottesville address served two purposes: that Roosevelt with this speech was putting out feelers to see what the American people would accept, and that he was also beginning the process of education so urgently needed in this period. His imagery was graphic and unmistakable:

Some indeed still hold to the now somewhat obvious delusion that we of the United States can safely permit the United States to become a lone island, a lone island in a world dominated by the philosophy of force.

Such an island may be the dream of those who still talk and vote as isolationists. Such an island represents to me and to the overwhelming majority of Americans today a helpless nightmare of a people without freedom—the nightmare of a people lodged in prison, handcuffed, hungry, and fed through the bars from day to day by the contemptuous, unpitying masters of other continents.[22]

The decision announced at Charlottesville—that all-out aid to the Allies was to be regarded by the administration as equally important to equipping ourselves — was based on Roosevelt's belief that Britain would be able to hold out. Roosevelt had long had his own doubts about the internal strength of France, and from the time of the Nazi breakthrough at Sedan, five days after the May 10 attack on France, the administration was most dubious about France's ability to survive. The isolationists at the time were saying that both Britain and France were certain to go under and that we should therefore concentrate on our own defenses rather than dissipate our strength by sending them aid, and even some of Roosevelt's nonisolationist military and civilian advisers agreed.[23] But Roosevelt was never in doubt about Britain.[24] Undoubtedly the fact that the fighting Churchill had been called upon to form a new government there on May 10 influenced the President's thinking in this regard. Davis and Lindley, who were very close to the administration in these days, report that

Mr. Roosevelt based his confidence in England on two observable factors and one less tangible. His study of the reports of Dunkirk convinced him that the RAF had qualitative superiority over the *Luftwaffe.* He knew something about the advantages of a defense in depth and was assured that the British command, husbanding their numerical inferiority in the air, would take full advantage of that. Secondly, he found no evidence that the Nazis had accumulated the multitude of small craft necessary to transport sufficient men and equipment across the English Channel against formidable air and sea power. A navy man, Mr. Roosevelt also reposed considerable confidence in English seamanship—a confidence justified at Dunkirk. On the political side, he had faith in the tenacity and coolheadedness of the British. That faith was yet to be justified, it should be remembered, when the President announced the policy of all aid to the Allies and determined to put the destroyers in their hands.

Subsequently, White House optimism was re-enforced by the judgment of Colonel William J. Donovan, . . . the first expert visitor [to England] in the summer of 1940 to give the English more than a fifty-fifty chance, reporting to the President that they could hold out.[25]

Donovan did not return from London until early in August, however, by which time Roosevelt was well ahead on his own plans to aid Britain, plans based on his optimistic faith in her survival. This type of optimism and confidence, necessarily predicated in part on intangibles, is a most important aspect of the Rooseveltian captaincy in a crisis situation. His daughter Anna has remarked that the President considered confidence to be the very essence of leadership, that belief in one's cause, in this case belief in the inner strength of Britain, was necessary in order to be a good leader and a good strategist.[26]

Once he had quickly made his conclusions about Britain, the only question for the President was what, specifically, he might do to aid her. If any blueprint were needed, Churchill had furnished one which left no doubt as to what Britain wanted. Five days after assuming his new role as Prime Minister, he had sent Roosevelt a lengthy cable, which read in part:

But I trust you realise, Mr. President, that the voice and force of the United States may count for nothing if they are withheld too long. You may have a completely subjugated, Nazified Europe established with astonishing swiftness, and the weight may be more than we can bear. All I ask now is that you should proclaim nonbelligerency, which would mean that you would help us with everything short of actually engaging armed forces. Immediate needs are: First of all, the loan of forty or fifty of your older destroyers. . . . Secondly, we want several hundred of the latest types of aircraft, of which you are now getting delivery. These can be repaid by those now being constructed in the United States for us. Thirdly, anti-aircraft equipment and ammunition, of which again there will be plenty next year, if we are alive to see it. Fourthly, the fact that our ore supply is being compromised from Sweden, from North Africa, and perhaps from Northern Spain, makes it necessary to purchase steel in the United States. This also applies to other materials. We shall go on paying dollars for as long as we can, but I should like to feel reasonably sure that when we can pay no more, you will give us the stuff all the same. . . . [27]

The question of turning fifty destroyers over to Britain became the major focus of interest in the administration in the summer of 1940. In the task of convincing public opinion of the rightness of this move, Roosevelt had the help, once more, of his good friend William Allen White, heading a new organization, the Committee to Defend America by Aiding the Allies. Formation of a new committee, for the purpose of shaking the American people from their complacency about the European war, had been contemplated by White and Eichelberger as early as January 1940. They had sought and received administration approval for their plan. The events of April and May, however, did more than any words could have done to put an end to public lethargy. At the same time, those events made it all the more necessary to create an organization which might help to crystallize public opinion, now, in support of all-out aid to Britain and France. Thus the Committee to Defend America by Aiding the Allies (henceforth shortened to CDAAA), in the making during the months of April and May, was formally announced on May 20. Over the next few months it became, in the words of Wayne Cole, "something of an unofficial public relations organization for President Roosevelt's foreign policy." White himself described his association with Roosevelt in the following way: "My relationship to President Roosevelt had been more of a morganatic relationship. I knew I had his private support. . . . I never did anything the President didn't ask for, and I always conferred with him on our program."[28]

The committee's headquarters was located in New York, Eichelberger's base and the city regarded as the country's internationalist center, but the committee itself was nationwide. By July 1 it had three hundred local chapters, established in every state of the Union except North Dakota, with a good deal of energy and capacity in those chapters located in major cities.[29] It was felt that the midwesterner, generally thought to be the most isolationist-minded in the country, would be the hardest to reach, but the fact that William Allen White was chairman of the CDAAA was considered an enormous asset in this regard.

Roosevelt himself had made his own effort to awaken this section of the country by pointing out, in his May 16 speech, that in an air age midwesterners could not consider themselves immune from attack simply because they were removed from the two coasts. Describing the possibilities, he had warned:

The islands off the west coast of Africa are only 1,500 miles from Brazil. Modern planes starting from the Cape Verde Islands can be over Brazil in seven hours.

And Para, Brazil, near the mouth of the Amazon River, is but four flying-hours to Caracas, Venezuela; and Venezuela is but two and one-half hours to Cuba and the Canal Zone; and Cuba and the Canal Zone are two and one-quarter hours to Tampico, Mexico; and Tampico is two and one-quarter hours to St. Louis, Kansas City and Omaha.[30]

It is interesting to note that the administration had been contemplating for quite some time an appeal to the Midwest in this fashion. In a draft of a speech found in the Roosevelt files, dated November 8, 1939, appears the following passage:

Suppose you who dwell in the South or the Middlewest look at your geography book again. A hostile air base in Yucatan is only a short hop from there to Mobile or New Orleans or Galveston or Houston.

It is only a matter of ―― hours for an enemy squadron of bombers to go from Yucatan or from Tampico all the way up to St. Louis or Kansas City, or many other large and prosperous communities lying on the Mississippi River or its tributaries.[31]

The inference in appeals of this sort was that midwesterners, too, would be very short-sighted in not wanting to assure a victory by England and France.

Now, in June, it was too late to expect to save France, which indeed capitulated on June 22. But seven days later Roosevelt and William Allen White were seriously discussing the possibility of sending U.S. destroyers to Britain, with Roosevelt suggesting that they might be swapped for bases on British island possessions in this hemisphere. The linking of destroyers with bases, White's biographer hastens to point out, was Roosevelt's own idea, and not White's.[32] After White's June 29 meeting with the President, the CDAAA began to concentrate its efforts on getting release of fifty or sixty U.S. destroyers to Britain. Its method was to build up public opinion in support of this step, thus giving positive proof to the White House that the country wanted this done.[33]

If the CDAAA seemed to pressure Roosevelt, it was a kind of pressure that he welcomed, for he very much wanted to accomplish the destroyer transaction. It would not be a simple matter. Although the United States was now supplying Britain with aircraft, guns, and other vital war materials, this was being done through existing legal channels, by means of government sale or transfer to private manufacturers, who in turn sold the materials to Britain after they had been declared "surplus" by the U.S. military. After the British had been forced to leave all their equipment on the beaches of Dunkirk, the United States went far toward depleting its own arsenals to resupply Britain's army. However, the alienation of fifty destroyers from our own navy, traditionally America's "first line of defense," would be a step of such startling magnitude that it had to be very carefully considered. In addition to the effect it would have upon public opinion, there were also serious and baffling legal obstacles to such a move. On the statute books the Espionage Act of 1917 and the newly enacted Walsh Act of June 28, 1940 prohibited the turning over of United States ships necessary to defense to a belligerent.

For a while, during the month of July, Roosevelt resisted pressure from various interventionists to go ahead with the transfer. He was concerned that there would be a public outcry against the sending of destroyers, as there had not been in the case of planes,[34] and, troubled by what he felt to be legal restrictions, he hesitated to act without more explicit authority from Congress. However, to go to Congress would precipitate a prolonged and bitter debate on the eve of the presidential political campaign.[35]

Meanwhile, British shipping losses were mounting. By the end of

July nearly half of the one hundred British destroyers available for home waters were lost or damaged, and Churchill made his third request to Roosevelt (the first two had been sent on May 15 and June 11) for "old" destroyers. His cable to the President read, in part, as follows:

Latterly the air attack on our shipping has become injurious. In the last ten days we have had the following destroyers sunk: *Brazen, Codrington, Delight, Wren,* and the following damaged: *Beagle, Boreas, Brilliant, Griffin, Montrose, Walpole, Whitshed*; total eleven. All this in the advent of any attempt which may be made at invasion! Destroyers are frightfully vulnerable to air-bombing, and yet they must be held in the air-bombing area to prevent sea-borne invasion. We could not sustain the present rate of casualties for long, and if we cannot get a substantial reinforcement the whole fate of the war may be decided by this minor and easily remediable factor.

This is a frank account of our present situation, and I am confident, now that you know exactly how we stand, that you will leave nothing undone to ensure that fifty or sixty of your oldest destroyers are sent to me at once. I can fit them very quickly with Asdics and use them against U-boats on the western approaches, and so keep the more modern and better-gunned craft for the Narrow Seas against invasion. Mr. President, with great respect I must tell you that in the long history of the world this is a thing to do *now.* Large construction is coming to me in 1941, but the crisis will be reached long before 1941. I know you will do all in your power, but I feel entitled and bound to put the gravity and urgency of the position before you.[36]

Churchill's cable was sent on July 31. At a cabinet meeting on August 2 the destroyer issue was extensively discussed. Roosevelt was by now thoroughly committed to going through with the transfer, and the cabinet discussion focused on the question of methods. It was decided that the newly nominated Republican presidential candidate, Wendell Willkie, should be approached, through William Allen White, with a request for help in persuading Republican congressional leaders to support new legislation making the transfer possible. Willkie, when asked, indicated to White that although he sympathized with what Roosevelt was attempting to do he was unwilling to be a go-between in appealing to the Republican leadership.[37]

Determined, the President took the next course open to him. The White House got word to one of its most active supporters, Senator Claude Pepper, that it was contemplating a destroyers-for-bases exchange, and asked Pepper to speak to Charles McNary, leader of the Republican forces in the Senate. McNary was among those moderate isolationists who were themselves alarmed after the fall of

France. McNary's answer to Pepper was that in the event the issue were raised in Congress he would have to vote against it, but if the administration found another way to effect the transfer, he would not speak against it on the floor of the Senate.[38] Subsequently, one of the President's top advisers, Benjamin V. Cohen, who had been actively trying all summer to find a way to persuade Roosevelt that there was a legal basis for accomplishing the destroyer transaction within existing legislation, now bent his great legal talent to the effort once more and, together with Dean Acheson, fashioned a long and cogently argued opinion that was published in the *New York Times* on Sunday, August 11, over the signatures of four distinguished lawyers—Dean Acheson himself, Acheson's partner George Rublee, Charles C. Burlingham, and Thomas D. Thacher. It was at this point that Roosevelt began to feel that the destroyer deal might be accomplished even without new legislation.[39]

While proceeding to make arrangements with the British, Roosevelt, continuing to deal cautiously with public opinion and with Congress, also carefully watched the home front. He sanctioned the delivery of an important address by Bullitt, newly returned from France, in order to gauge public opinion. On August 13 Roosevelt approved a draft of the speech that Bullitt delivered to the American Philosophical Society in Philadelphia on August 18. The speech contained an explicit warning of what would happen if the United States failed to stand fast with England in order to thwart Hitler's principle of picking off one enemy at a time. "It is my conviction," Bullitt said,

drawn from my own experience and from the information in the hands of our government in Washington, that the United States is in as great peril today as was France a year ago. And I believe that unless we act now, decisively, to meet the threat we shall be too late.

The dictators are convinced that all democracies will always be too late. You remember Hitler's statement: "Each country will imagine that it alone will escape. I shall not even need to destroy them one by one. Selfishness and lack of foresight will prevent each one fighting until it is too late."

Although isolationist reaction to Bullitt's speech was strongly critical and outraged, the overall public response was overwhelmingly favorable.[40]

In dealing with Congress, Roosevelt needed not only to watch the Republicans but also Democratic Senator David I. Walsh, chairman of the Senate Naval Affairs Committee. The isolationist Irishman

from Massachusetts had openly declared that the transfer of destroyers from our flag would be an act of war. By inviting Walsh to spend
a weekend aboard the presidential yacht and by afterward replying
to his objections in a lengthy letter, containing a strong personal
appeal, Roosevelt managed, if not to convince Walsh, at least to keep
him from publicly raising objections when the destroyers-bases swap
was announced.[41]

On September 3, Congress and the press were simultaneously
informed of the completion of the destroyers-for-bases transfer by
executive agreement. Congress was, as Roosevelt stressed in his press
conference of September 3, presented with a fait accompli. The
justifications given Congress and the press were the same that
Roosevelt had stressed with Senator Walsh—that acquisition of bases
would greatly strengthen our national defense, that the trading of
fifty overage destroyers for these vital naval and air bases was a good
bargain, and that there had been a precedent set for such solo action
by the President in Jefferson's purchase of Louisiana.[42] Because the
ring of bases, acquired in the British Crown colonies of Newfoundland, Bermuda, the Bahamas, Jamaica, St. Lucia, Trinidad, Antigua,
and British Guiana, would afford vital protection for the Western
Hemisphere, Admiral Stark, Chief of Naval Operations, was able
technically to comply with the Walsh Act by certifying that the
destroyers were not essential to the national security. The linkage
with bases also stole some of the isolationists' thunder, for they had
long been advocating such acquisitions as payments for war debts.
Even the most vocally isolationist organ of the Midwest, the *Chicago
Tribune*, praised the deal, saying: "THE TRIBUNE rejoices to make
this announcement, which fulfills a policy advocated by this
newspaper since 1922. . . . THE TRIBUNE persisted, month by
month and year by year, in calling for these additions to the national
defense . . . . The agreement is not in the terms THE TRIBUNE
would have preferred. Nevertheless, any arrangement which gives the
United States naval and air bases in regions which must be brought
within the American defense zone is to be accepted as a triumph."[43]

The destroyer deal, later termed by Churchill, "a decidedly
unneutral act," represented a certain gamble for Roosevelt. Not the
gamble of war, for both he and Churchill were convinced that Hitler
was not yet ready to declare war on the United States and would not
use this as an excuse to do so.[44] Yet the President gambled with the
possibility that this would ignite the old charge that he was acting

dictatorially, with little respect for the laws or the Constitution. The elaborate argument that there was a precedent in Jefferson's purchase of Louisiana was an attempt to prove the legality of the destroyer transfer, about which Roosevelt himself had had many doubts. This was an election year, in which, Roosevelt thought, the greatest issue would be the third term break with precedent.[45] If that proved to be so, any act which might give more fuel to the charge of "dictator" could be dangerous.

It is not surprising, therefore, that Roosevelt, perhaps in a bleak moment, remarked to Colonel "Wild Bill" Donovan that he expected to lose the election on this issue.[46] It is doubtful that Roosevelt remained this pessimistic for very long, but his remark is indicative of the fact that he felt a grave political gamble was involved. Nevertheless, there would be a greater gamble in refusing England's request for destroyers, for to Roosevelt, as well as to Churchill, it had come down to a question of survival, of Britain's continuance in the war and, ultimately, of the survival of the United States. While drafting his message to Congress, the President had said to his secretary Grace Tully that "even another day's delay may mean the end of civilization. Cries of 'warmonger' and 'dictator' will fill the air, but if Britain is to survive, we must act."[47]

The fifty reconditioned World War I destroyers did yeoman service in the British navy, but at least equally important was the psychological value to the British people of such a gesture on the eve of the most punishing phase of the Battle of Britain. The ships were tangible proof of Roosevelt's faith in British staying power and of his determination to fulfill the Charlottesville pledge.

5

A VOTE OF CONFIDENCE, OF SORTS

In mid-1941 the American journalist Raymond Gram Swing declared in an article written for the London *Sunday Express*: "The great agitation in the United States today is over the President's leadership. He is being snarled at, shouted at, prayed at, blasted at, to tell the country the whole truth, and to lead the nation right off into convoying, which is a new word meaning war. The President's closest friends are the most impatient. . . . One catchword of the hour is that the President is behind public opinion, that in not leading it, he may lose it, and the opinion may turn against and drift off, say to Lindbergh and the appeasers."[1] Even before 1941 the more internationalist minded had claimed that the President was not giving proper leadership. The feeling in those circles, in the long two-year period before Pearl Harbor, was that Roosevelt alone could furnish the necessary leadership, that if he spoke out the myriad of confusing voices would be hushed and the issues at last clarified. But in 1939 Roosevelt had felt that the time was not yet ripe for the clarifying of issues. Events had first to impress themselves upon the people before he could serve as the proper interpreter of those events. Even after the 1940 blitzkrieg, however, he continued to exercise caution in his public statements. A few hours prior to the Charlottesville address William Allen White wired Roosevelt: "My correspondence is heaping up unanimously behind the plan to aid the Allies by anything other than war. As an old friend, let me warn you

70

that maybe you will not be able to lead the American people unless you catch up with them. They are going fast."[2]

Charlottesville was that strong call to action desired by White and the type of internationalist White represented, who wanted all aid to Britain short of war. Following the June 10 address, however, there were no more presidential statements of that nature until the September 3 press conference announcing the destroyers-for-bases transfer. But behind the scenes Roosevelt was doing what he felt necessary and what, incidentally, also happened to coincide with the desires of all but the most rabid interventionists, those who now wanted an outright declaration of war. For the most part, he was taking action without broadcasting it, as he explained in a letter of June 7 to former budget director Lewis Douglas, in answer to a critical letter from Douglas:

Dear Lew:

I beat you to it! Very many planes are actually on the way to the Allies, deliveries to this Government being put off. . . . We are turning in old Army and Navy materiel to the manufacturers who have been given orders for new and up-to-date materiel. I have a sneaking suspicion that the old materiel which we are turning in will be on its way to France in a few days.

Actually I am adopting the thought ["policy" was crossed out on the original copy of the letter and the word "thought" written in in longhand] that the more effective immediately usable materiel we can get to the other side will mean the destruction of an equivalent amount of German materiel—thereby aiding American defense in the long run.

So you see I am doing everything possible—though I am not talking very much about it because a certain element of the Press, like the Scripps-Howard papers, would undoubtedly pervert it, attack it and confuse the public mind. This is inadvisable even though I am personally well accustomed to it.[3]

In the case of the destroyer deal, as indicated in the preceding chapter, Roosevelt was working out the ways and means in his own mind during the summer of 1940 while at the same time encouraging public opinion organizers such as William Allen White to stimulate public attitudes in favor of such a transaction. Fully aware of Britain's perilous position that summer, he did not need to be prodded by public opinion in order to take necessary action. His letter to Douglas shows that he was apt to be "doing everything possible" on his own accord. Although Langer and Gleason have given the credit for the destroyers-for-bases deal to an organized public pressuring the President, saying that "Mr. Roosevelt's way had been carefully prepared by those organizations which not only plotted a safe course for him but also carried the burden of public education,"[4] the impetus for such public pressure came more from Roosevelt than from any other single source.

The tactics which Roosevelt used in rallying public opinion in support of the destroyer swap he was to resort to again and again throughout the following year and a half before Pearl Harbor. For the most part, the approach to the public was indirect. While considering a certain course that might be necessary, he would encourage others to speak out forcefully ahead of him, and so prepare the way for his own statements and actions. He would not commit himself, however, until he was fully determined upon the action, in effect always leaving his options open until the point of decision. At the point of commitment, he could be relied upon for as strong a statement as was necessary—the kind of statement he had made in the Charlottesville speech and would make again in the famous Arsenal of Democracy address at the end of 1940, the address which would call for the far-reaching program of Lend-Lease aid to the Allies.

Not only did he encourage private citizens to stimulate public opinion but he was not averse to having members of his own official family speak out ahead of him, taking positions in advance of his own. Sometimes an official's speech might serve as a trial balloon, as had the Bullitt speech of August 18. At another time a speech might merely serve to enlighten public opinion and thereby create the kind of climate in which the President could act forcefully. The more sensitive observers of Roosevelt were not unaware of what he was doing, and words of praise came from no less a person than the British sovereign, who, in the very midst of Britain's critical period, was quite satisfied with the way Roosevelt was conducting foreign policy on this side of the Atlantic. George VI, certain after their talks in 1939 that he had been given particular insights into the President's mind, wrote him a letter in mid-1941 that revealed an appreciation of the subtleties of Roosevelt's leadership of public opinion. "I have read with great interest," the King reported, "all that you have said & done during the past months, since you have been re-elected President, & I have been so struck by the way you have led public opinion by allowing it to get ahead of you."[5]

Within his own official family at least one cabinet officer, Harold Ickes, could be relied upon to take an outspokenly strong foreign policy position, ahead of the President's, and when Roosevelt brought Frank Knox and Henry L. Stimson into his cabinet, on June

20, 1940, he was assuring himself of two more loudly interventionist speakers. Knox came in as Secretary of the Navy, replacing Acting Secretary Charles A. Edison, and Stimson, as Secretary of War, replaced the isolationist Harry Woodring. Both men had taken positions well in advance of Roosevelt's public stand for quite some time. By coincidence, both had made speeches as recently as June 18, the evening before they had been asked to join the Roosevelt administration, speeches in which they had proclaimed very advanced ideas. Knox had come out in favor of the compulsory draft and for American control of the Atlantic, perhaps in cooperation with the British. Stimson, who as early as March 6, 1939 had called for a direct military understanding between the United States, Great Britain, and France to stop Hitler, had advocated repeal of the neutrality legislation, the opening of American ports for repair and servicing of British ships, and, if necessary, American convoying of supplies to Britain. And, like Knox, he had also spoken on June 18 in favor of compulsory military training.[6] Significantly, when Stimson was asked the next day to join Roosevelt's cabinet and in return queried the President as to whether he fully understood and approved of the Stimson position, the response was entirely in the affirmative. As Stimson recorded in his Diary:

About seven P.M. I telephoned the President and asked him three questions: (1) Whether he had seen my radio speech and whether it would be embarrassing to him. He replied that he had already read it and was in full accord with it. (2) I asked him whether he knew that I was in favor of general compulsory military service, and he said he did and gave me to understand that he was in sympathy with me. (3) I asked him whether Knox had accepted and he said he had. I then accepted.[7]

Stimson and Knox represented a new type of support that Roosevelt was receiving in the post-Munich years, the support of anti-New Deal people who were at the same time in favor of a strongly interventionist foreign policy. White House mail in these years abounds with such comments as the following, sent to Roosevelt in early 1939 from an old acquaintance at Campobello:

I cannot resist writing to you and expressing my sincere admiration for your honest, practical and realistic foreign policy.

In as much as practically every single act of the "New Deal" has set me in a fine frenzy from which I shall never recover this letter can not be considered as coming from a chronic supporter of Administration acts. I do know, however, that if you can overcome the combination in the Congress of wishful pacifists and ignorant isolationists and establish our foreign policy firmly along the lines of your present aims you will have done a service to America and the world at large that will justify your place in history among our very great. (In spite of the New Deal.)[8]

While the years immediately preceding the fall of France saw a great many liberals adamantly opposed to the United States adopting a bellicose position in world affairs, Roosevelt picked up support in these years from anti-liberal sections—the conservative South, for instance—and from the Frank Knox type of Republican, strongly antilabor and antiliberal, who also tended toward militancy in foreign policy.[9]

There were other considerations, in addition to the fact that Stimson and Knox strengthened the interventionist position in the cabinet, that prompted the appointment of these two Republicans. Living so close to the Wilson era and having been himself a member of the Wilson administration, Roosevelt was extremely conscious of the Wilsonian mistakes and was determined not to repeat them. Roosevelt's tendency to think always in political terms caused him to concentrate on what he undoubtedly considered Wilson's greatest mistake, his failure to make his foreign policy a bipartisan one. Upon the outbreak of the Second World War, therefore, the President sought to avoid this past error by including prominent Republicans within his cabinet, and thought of bringing in both Republican candidates on the presidential ticket in 1936, Landon and Knox. He discussed the idea with Ickes, who recorded the following conversation, of September 6, 1939, in his Diary:

Then he went on to say that the columnists had been harping on the idea that there should be taken into the Administration such men as Herbert Hoover, Vandenberg, Taft, young Lodge, and "even Dewey." He observed: "Of course, I understand what all this means," and I interrupted with: "It means that they are trying to build up a Republican candidate for next year." "Exactly," said the President. ["] They do not say anything about Landon and Knox, the titular heads of the Republican party.["] I asked him if he knew Knox well because I had with me a long, two-page letter from Frank to show to the President and I had it in mind to suggest to him that he might well consider taking Knox into the Cabinet. The President replied that he did not know him well and then I said that while he was impetuous and inclined to think off the top of his head at times, he liked the President personally, he was loyal, and I thought that he would do a good job if called upon. His attitude on the international situation has been as fine as anyone could ask for.

The President had been thinking about the possibility of bringing both Landon and Knox into the Cabinet, and he asked me what I thought of it. I thought well of it and told him so.[10]

Very shortly the enthusiasm for Landon cooled,[11] but Roosevelt continued to think of the possibility of bringing Knox in. In December 1939, following the death of Secretary of the Navy Swanson, he offered him the post. Knox's letter to Roosevelt, written immediately after their White House meeting on December 10, reveals the substance of their conversation and the political considerations which weighed heavily with both men. "I am sending this letter to you," Knox wrote the President on December 15,

through the kindness of Mr. Paul Leach in order that it may evade the evident leaks which followed our last talk. . . .

I know you will believe me when I say that I have been giving very conscientious, indeed, almost prayerful, consideration to the matter we discussed. . . .

I am also keenly conscious of the great compliment you paid me in asking me to become a member of your official family, despite the fact that I have been one of the most active, and I fear sometimes cantankerous, critics of your domestic program. May I add that it is also even more a tribute to your broad gauged patriotism that you should seriously consider such action.

As I explained to you, the only things that give me pause are the absence at the moment on the part of the public of any deep sense of crisis which would justify completely forgetting and obliterating party lines, and the fact that the addition of only one Republican to the Cabinet would not make it, in the public view, a coalition cabinet into which a member of the opposition could go without encountering overwhelming criticism which would be destructive of any reputation one may have built through a whole lifetime of pretty consistent party loyalty. I was delighted to observe on Sunday your prompt recognition of the cogency of this argument.[12]

Knox suggested his good friend, Colonel William J. "Wild Bill" Donovan, as the second Republican for the cabinet. Although Roosevelt was ready and willing to take Knox, who had been a Rough Rider and a lifelong friend of Theodore Roosevelt and who could be expected to work well with the second Roosevelt, there was some doubt as to whether Donovan would prove loyal.[13] Roosevelt could tolerate, and even welcome, differing political viewpoints within his own official family, but his one criterion for service within his administration was devotion to himself.[14] He hedged on the Donovan suggestion, therefore, writing to Knox in none too candid a fashion:

Bill Donovan is also an old friend of mine—we were in the law school together—and, frankly, I should like to have him in the Cabinet, not only for his own ability, but also to repair in a sense the very great injustice done him by President Hoover in the Winter of 1929. [Hoover had received strong support from Donovan in 1928 and had promised him a cabinet post, but, after winning the election, failed to appoint him.] Here again the question of motive must be considered, and I fear that to put two Republicans in charge of the armed forces might be misunderstood in both parties!

So let us let the whole matter stand as it is for a while. If things continue as they are today and there is a stalemate or what might be called a normal course of war in Europe, I take it we shall have an old fashioned hot and bitter campaign this Summer and Autumn. Such campaigns—viewing with alarm and pointing with pride—are a little stupid and a little out of date, and their appeal to prejudice does little to encourage a more intelligent electorate. . . .

On the other hand, if there should develop a real crisis . . . it would be necessary to put aside in large part strictly old fashioned party government, and the people would understand such a situation. If this develops I want you to know that I would still want you as a part of such an Administration. Also, I hope much that you will run down to see me from time to time to talk over events as they occur. In this job I need every angle from every part of the country.[15]

Having left the door ajar, Roosevelt in the midst of the "real crisis" telephoned, on June 19, 1940, both Knox and another prominent Republican, Henry L. Stimson, who had served as Secretary of War and Secretary of State in Republican administrations. The next day, June 20, the announcement was made that the two war posts in the cabinet would henceforth be handled by these two men.[16] Although he was accused of playing politics on the eve of the Republican convention, the President had intended to form a coalition cabinet long before the step was finally taken. The June 20 announcement may have been dramatic, but it was just one more instance of Roosevelt's carefully thought out, responsible moves in this prewar period.

While internationalist organizations and forceful cabinet members might push for a stronger foreign policy, and while the American people in general were being stirred out of their apathy by events in Europe in the spring and summer of 1940, at the same time the isolationists, albeit somewhat reduced in numbers, were closing ranks in an organized fashion to form the America First Committee. When the public opinion expert Hadley Cantril came to the conclusion, in September 1940, that isolationist sentiment in the United States was then limited to one-quarter of the populace, the attitudes he attributed to this segment happened to be very much like those of most of the leaders of the America First movement. Cantril found that about one-quarter of the total population thinks that it is more important for the United States to keep out of war than to help England, and at the same time believes either that we should do less or at least no more to help England than we are now doing. Although most of these people believe that Germany will win the war, they tend to think a German victory would not disturb their own lives or the security of this country.[17]

Wayne Cole, author of the definitive study of the America First Committee, explicitly defined its outlook when he explained:

America First Committee leaders did not believe Hitler could successfully invade Great Britain. Nor did they believe that Britain could defeat Hitler without the full military participation of the United States in the war.

. . .

But even if England fell they believed the United States with its free labor and capitalistic system could successfully compete with German slave labor and National Socialism in world trade. . . . America First leaders . . . believed even if an Axis victory reduced foreign trade, it would be less harmful to the American economy than intervention in the war. They believed substitutes and synthetic products could be developed to compensate for materials which might not be available because of Axis controls.[18]

And, Cole added:

Even if Hitler were completely victorious over England, they did not believe he would attempt an invasion of the Western Hemisphere. They did not base this stand upon any faith in Hitler's promises. They believed the difficulty of the task would deter even the fanatic Hitler from attempting it.[19]

These suppositions were the very opposite of Roosevelt's, who was firmly convinced that Hitler, if successful against England, would constitute both an economic and strategic threat to this hemisphere.

The "isolationists," or "noninterventionists," as they were less frequently called in this prewar period, organized the America First Committee in order to counter the activities of the Committee to Defend America by Aiding the Allies. In the making since July 1940, America First was officially announced on September 4, the day after the destroyer deal was made public. Chicago, considered the center of isolationist sentiment in the country,[20] was its head-quarters and nearly two-thirds of the committee's membership could be found within a three-hundred mile radius of the Windy City. America Firsters were preceded by smaller noninterventionist organizations, such as Father Coughlin's Christian Front, William Dudley Pelley's Silver Shirts, the American Peace Mobilization, and the

Citizens to Keep America Out of War Committee, some of whom the America First Committee would work with. The larger committee, more representative of majority isolationist sentiment, made an effort, however, not always successful or consistent, to keep out the radical fringe element.[21]

America First's official position was responsibly temperate. Its first statement of principles, given out at the same time as the public announcement of the committee's formation, read as follows:

1. The United States must built an impregnable defense for America.
2. No foreign power, no group of powers, can successfully attack a *prepared* America.
3. American democracy can be preserved only by keeping out of the European war.
4. "Aid short of war" weakens national defense at home and threatens to involve America in war abroad.[22]

All-out aid to Britain, they feared, would bring America into the war, but after a while a revised statement of principles proclaimed that some aid to Britain might be considered, with proper limitations. In a country where the overwhelming sympathy of the people was with the British, even America Firsters, although many were anglophobic, hastened to declare that they hoped Britain would not be defeated. However, they consistently denied that England's fight was America's fight, and, convinced that Britain could not defeat Germany without American armed intervention, urged a negotiated peace in Europe.[23]

The committee's concentration was almost exclusively upon the European war, thus reflecting the attitudes of most Americans, who tended in this pre-Pearl Harbor period to feel, as their government did, that the Far Eastern situation was of secondary importance. Whenever they did consider the Orient, however, Americans were much less inclined to take an isolationist posture. Attitudes were colored in part by a traditional sympathy for China, but also by a strong and prevalent racism in the United States. The American people felt that the Japanese, a yellow race, would be easier to defeat than the Teutonic. Eric Goldman, cogently summarizing the views of the Midwest in particular and of Americans in general, has written:

In the vast span of middle states swinging from the Canadian to the Mexican borders, millions of Americans had been isolationist or little interested in international affairs. But their attitude was isolationism or indifferentism with a twist. They responded little to Europe; . . . and shied away from fighting in its wars. Yet in many cases they were not only willing but eager to be involved with Asia. The habit of thinking reached a temporary climax at the time of Pearl Harbor. Significantly, the influential Chicago *Tribune*, savage opponent of FDR's "finaglings in Europe," swung happily behind the war in Asia, "our natural area."

... Many long-time developments are entangled in the attitude: the fact that most Americans came from families who left Europe by a deliberate act of rejection; the participation in transatlantic wars which left millions sure that they had been "suckered"; an anxiety about the "hordes" of Asia and an assumption of superiority to yellow peoples—feelings which in combination inclined Americans to believe that they need not fear dealing with Asia and that they had better do it; ... and the long-pervasive influence of American missionaries and traders who crossed the Pacific. Just because of the many strands that went into it, the attitude had particular emotional potency.[24]

Pearl Buck found American racist attitudes so pronounced that she was moved to send the following prescient warning to Mrs. Eleanor Roosevelt immediately after Pearl Harbor:

... we must remember that there is in all the Oriental peoples a very deep sense that the white man generally is, or may be, their common enemy, and that in the final analysis it remains always a possibility that the point may come when these peoples, even such present enemies as the Chinese and the Japanese, may unite as colored against white.... It may be best expressed by a remark made lately by a Chinese professor, "Although the Japanese are our enemies just now, if it came to the ultimate choice, we would rather be a dependency of Japan than of the United States, because at least the Japanese do not consider us an inferior race.[25]

While the isolationists worked mainly through the America First Committee, the "internationalists" or "interventionists" were dividing into two major pressure groups, with distinctly different attitudes. The Committee to Defend America by Aiding the Allies reflected White's determination that all aid should be given England short of war. In the early summer of 1940 a more advanced cadre of interventionists formed informally and because they were accustomed to meeting at the Century Association in New York, a private club, became known as the Century Group. They shared some of their membership with the White Committee, with whom they frequently collaborated. The Century Group was convinced, however, that sooner or later the United States would have to enter the war to prevent world domination by Hitler, and it was dedicated to bringing America, by a series of steps leading to further and further involvement with Britain, to this position. This was entirely opposite to William Allen White's hope and desire that all-out aid to the Allies would be sufficient to preclude the necessity of U.S. entry into the war.[26] Later, the more advanced interventionist faction gained strength even with the White Committee, and White felt it necessary to resign his chairmanship at the end of 1940.[27]

Together, the White Committee and the Century Group reflected the viewpoints of most of the population, who by midsummer of 1940 were interventionist in varying degrees. Interpreting the polls, Hadley Cantril found that one-third of the populace was strongly interventionist. Their beliefs, paralleling those of the Century Group, Cantril defined as follows:

These people believe it is more important to help England, even at the risk of war, than it is for this country to keep out of war. They also think that we should do more that we are now doing to help England. Unlike the isolationists, they do not feel immune to the consequences of a Nazi victory, either as individuals or as members of a nation.[28]

Cantril's "interventionists" slighly outnumbered the "isolationists," whom he found to be one-fourth of the population by the summer of 1940. The "interventionists" themselves were slightly outnumbered by those whom Cantril termed "sympathetic." He found this latter group composed "almost 40 per cent of the total population," which, he said, "fear . . . the consequences of a German victory" yet "believe there is still hope for an English victory which can be brought about by the greater material help this country should provide England."[29] The views of the "sympathetic" group obviously coincided with the William Allen White position.

By the fall of 1940 there was a change in the relative strength of these three groupings. The isolationists were fewer in number while those who were willing to help England *even at the risk of war* had grown to approximately half of the population. In fact, polls taken from May 1940 on show a generally steady increase in the latter category, but with short periods of fluctuation in the fall of 1940 and again in the late spring of 1941. In August 1940, 47 percent of the people favored aid to England even at the risk of war. In September, that figure was up to 52 percent, but by October 1940, on the eve of the presidential election, the population was exactly divided: 50 percent favored aid at the risk of war while another 50 percent felt it was more important for the United States to stay out of war than to help England.[30]

Antiwar sentiment was certainly strong enough for a 1940

campaigner to have to be constantly aware of it. Roosevelt's campaign stance that year was comparable to Wilson's in 1916, and his appraisal of the wartime situation was also remarkably similar. As in the case of Wilson, Roosevelt presented himself as desirous of peace, while he harbored thoughts about his inability to keep America out of war. This kind of contradiction reflected the basic dilemma of the American people themselves in 1940-1941. From the time of the invasion of France, whenever the question was asked by pollsters: "Do you think the United States will go into the war in Europe sometime before it is over, or do you think we will stay out of the war?" a sizable majority thought we would go in.[31] But always on the direct question of voting for a declaration of war, the polls recorded an overwhelming majority of the people as opposed.

Foreign policy was bound to be a major concern of the people in 1940 as they voted for their President. The candidates, however, did little to clarify the issue. The Republican party was still the citadel of the isolationists, but the Republican standard-bearer, Wendell Willkie, happened to be an internationalist whose foreign policy position was practically identical to Roosevelt's. Willkie had supported the destroyers-for-bases deal in principle, although he had termed the President's method for effecting the transfer "arbitrary and dictatorial."[32] Willkie also favored the Selective Service Act of September 1940, authorizing the first peacetime draft in the nation's history. His line of attack upon Roosevelt early in the campaign was to charge that he did not adequately foresee or prepare for the present emergency. He held the President partly responsible both for the Munich appeasement and the fall of France, and he voiced the Republican party's accusation that the Roosevelt administration had neglected the defenses of the United States.[33] It was a telling argument, for in 1940 the United States was still in a sorry stage of unpreparedness. Although Congress had become thoroughly alarmed after the spring blitzkrieg and had then rapidly responded to Roosevelt's many requests for extraordinary defense appropriations, resulting by September in a total of $10.5 billion appropriated in the year 1940,[34] it would be many months before the effects of increased spending would become evident in delivery of weapons.

Yet the charge of neglect was also an easy one to counter politically, and on this score Roosevelt took the offensive by citing the records of Republicans in Congress before the spring blitz days. In his Madison Square Garden speech, on October 28, he quoted statements by isolationists such as Congressman Hamilton Fish (from

Roosevelt's home district in New York), ex-President Hoover, Senator Vandenberg, and Senator Robert A. Taft given out before 1940 and declaring that the United States was spending too much money on defense. "Until the present campaign opened," he charged, "Republican leaders, in and out of the Congress shouted from the housetops that our defenses were fully adequate."[35]

Roosevelt's own foreign policy position in the campaign was twofold: he reaffirmed the administration's policy of all possible aid to Britain and he reasserted his aversion to war. In a speech before the Teamsters Union convention on September 11 he said:

I hate war, now more than ever. I have one supreme determination—to do all that I can to keep war away from these shores for all time. I stand, with my party, and outside of my party as President of all the people, on the platform, the wording that was adopted in Chicago less than two months ago. It said:

We will not participate in foreign wars, and we will not send our Army, naval or air forces to fight in foreign lands outside of the Americas, except in case of attack.[36]

This phrase from the Democratic platform was repeated in subsequent campaign speeches, but in a speech in Boston, on October 30, a different emphasis was given. The Boston statement would henceforth be quoted time and again by those who would charge that Roosevelt was deliberately misleading the American people in this election campaign. That statement was an unequivocal pledge:

And while I am talking to you mothers and fathers, I give you one more assurance.

I have said this before, but I shall say it again and again and again:
Your boys are not going to be sent into any foreign wars.[37]

Willkie had changed his tactics in the closing weeks of the campaign and had resorted, on the advice of Republican professionals, to branding Roosevelt a warmonger and to charging that if Roosevelt were reelected American boys had best be prepared to board the transports. Roosevelt had therefore felt it necessary to come down heavily on the peace theme in the campaign finale, and he had indicated to a sympathetic Washington columnist on October 22 that he intended to do just that.[38] Even so, the President's speech writers have recorded that he was very hesitant to use the strong pledge incorporated into the Boston speech, and that he finally decided to do so at the urgings of the new Democratic national chairman, Ed Flynn, and his own speech writer, Robert Sherwood. After deciding on the wording, he then became testy with Rosenman, who reminded him that the platform had included the words, "except in case of attack," which were now being left out of this speech. Plainly Roosevelt did not like having to make the Boston pledge at all, and disliked discussing it any further with his writers.[39]

Very soon after his reelection Roosevelt sent a letter to Judge Rosenman which revealed some of his reasons for running and also, it would seem, attempted to justify any questionable campaign tactics.

Dear Sam,

Somehow, you and I made the same analysis of the votes on the fifth. In many ways, it was a narrow escape—not for personalities but for ideals. I wonder, with you, whether people will ever realize that. On Armistice Day, I tried to take the long-range view of the past and, at the same time, to imply that our type of civilization, though saved for a generation by the first World War, is again a world issue.

Furthermore, I have learned a number of things which make me shudder—because there were altogether too many people in high places in the Republican campaign who thought in terms of appeasement of Hitler—honest views most of them, and views based on the materialism in which they view not only themselves but their country.

So also in affairs at home, I live, as you know, in constant dread that the national security might, under remote circumstances, call for quick and drastic action. You and I have faced that possibility since 1928 and there have been a number of occasions when, both in Albany and Washington, it took real calm not to call out the troops. Little do people realize how I had to take abuse and criticism for inaction at the time of the Flint strike. I believed, and I was right, that the country including labor would learn the lesson of their own volition without having it forced upon them by marching troops.

No one can give guarantees for the future but I am certain that if the other crowd won there would have been many more probabilities of drastic action by the government. Those newspapers of the nation which most loudly cried dictatorship against me would have been the first to justify the beginnings of dictatorship by somebody else.[40]

Roosevelt's fear of dictatorial tactics throughout the country by an incoming Republican administration was undoubtedly ill-founded. An act of coercion must be the doing of a President rather than a party, and from what we know of Wendell Willkie he would have been no more willing to flout the democratic decencies than Roosevelt was. But the foreign policy issue was another matter. Willkie undoubtedly would have had great difficulty in controlling the strongly entrenched isolationist element within his own party, and in carrying the election it was likely that he would have even contributed to the reinforcement of those ranks. Therefore, it was imperative that Roosevelt should have won this election, in part because he had correctly judged himself the one person most capable of leading the nation successfully through the rigors of the Second World War and in part because his victory signified a triumph for internationalism as opposed to isolationism.

In the least confusing aspect of the campaign Roosevelt had managed to pin the isolationist label on the Republican party by often repeating in his campaign speeches the catchy phrase "Martin, Barton, and Fish." These three Republican Congressmen, Joe Martin, Hamilton Fish, and Bruce Barton, had had both a reactionary and isolationist voting pattern. Roosevelt indicted them in the Madison Square Garden speech of October 28 for their stand against repeal of the arms embargo. When he dwelt on the phrase and repeated it again in that speech, it made such an impression on radio audiences that two days later a Boston crowd responded as soon as he mentioned "Martin" by chanting with him "Barton and Fish." With the Boston and New York speeches carried on the national networks, the slogan caught on across the country, and the Republicans were implacably imbedded in the public mind as isolationists.[41] Voting patterns in the election tended to confirm that the interventionist vote went to Roosevelt.[42]

During the campaign Roosevelt had pledged, in his Columbus Day speech, that "no combination of dictator countries of Europe and Asia [Japan had just entered into an outright alliance with Germany and Italy with the Tripartite Pact of September 1940] will stop the help we are giving to almost the last free people now fighting to hold them at bay."[43] His next great step along the lines of all possible aid short of war would be Lend-Lease, but Roosevelt moved very hesitantly toward this gigantic new phase. Following the election, there was a procrastination of approximately two months, caused in part by the President's exhaustion after the campaign and also, in part, by his felt need to determine whether increased aid to Britain could be accomplished within existing legislation and whether Britain's dollar shortages had become as perilous as some of his advisers contended.[44]

When Roosevelt was at last convinced of the necessity for such a program, he himself conceived the idea of Lend-Lease[45] and presented it to the American people in two stages in the latter part of December. In his press conference of December 17 he explained:

Now, what I am trying to do is to eliminate the dollar sign. . . . get rid of the silly, foolish old dollar sign.

Well, let me give you an illustration: Suppose my neighbor's home catches fire, and I have a length of garden hose four or five hundred feet away. If he can take my garden hose and connect it up with his hydrant, I may help him to put out his fire. . . . He says, "All right, I will replace it." Now, if I get a nice garden hose back, I am in pretty good shape.

"With that neighborly analogy," Robert Sherwood has written, "Roosevelt won the fight for Lend Lease. There were to be two months of some of the bitterest debates in American history, but through it all the American people as a whole maintained the conviction that there couldn't be anything very radical or very dangerous in the President's proposal to lend our garden hose to the British. . . ."[46]

On December 29, a week and a half after the press conference, Roosevelt gave his next fireside chat, delivering the henceforth famous Arsenal of Democracy speech. In that speech, his strongest since the Charlottesville address, he once again painted an ominous geographical picture. "If Great Britain goes down," the President warned,

the Axis powers will control the continents of Europe, Asia, Africa, Australasia, and the high seas—and they will be in a position to bring enormous military and naval resources against this hemisphere. It is no exaggeration to say that all of us, in all the Americas, would be living at the point of a gun—a gun loaded with explosive bullets, economic as well as military.

To deal with this situation, Roosevelt recommended the following:

Thinking in terms of today and tomorrow, I make the direct statement to the American people that there is far less chance of the United States getting into war, if we do all we can now to support the nations defending themselves against attack by the Axis than if we acquiesce in their defeat, submit tamely to an Axis victory, and wait our turn to be the object of attack in another war later on.

He cautioned, however, that there was an element of risk in this proposal:

If we are to be completely honest with ourselves, we must admit that there is risk in any course we may take. But I deeply believe that the great majority of our people agree that the course that I advocate involves the least risk now and the greatest hope for world peace in the future.[47]

At the time, some observers commented that with the Arsenal of Democracy speech Roosevelt had at last presented clearly to the American people the risks involved in a program of all-out aid to Britain. The *Christian Science Monitor* wrote: "By ten o'clock on the night of December 29 . . . all the world knew that uncertainty no longer ruled. For President Roosevelt's fireside chat had clarified and crystallized America's choice, a choice really made long ago." Arthur Krock commented: "Candor, emerging at last from the camouflage of the campaign, has been received with a calmness which adds to the regret that this approach was delayed at the expense of six months of vital preparation."[48] Langer and Gleason conclude that "prior to the end of 1940 the American people had committed themselves to aiding the democracies by all means short of war. They were being asked in 1941 to commit themselves to aiding the democracies even at the risk of war."[49]

The administration, however, did not make the latter condition clear. On the contrary, it clouded that issue during the period of the "Great Debate" which followed hard upon the simultaneous introduction of the Lend-Lease bill in both houses of Congress on January 10, 1941. In principle Roosevelt was not averse to wide public debate on the measure, for, knowing he had the votes in Congress[50] and desiring more public support, he actually welcomed debate in the hope of gaining more than just passage of the Lend-Lease bill. Particularly concerned about divisions among the American people at this time, especially since he knew that a divided people could not fight a gigantic global war successfully, Roosevelt felt that in giving all sides a chance to air their views unity and concurrence in the final decision would be achieved, a unity vitally necessary not only for the successful implementation of the Lend-Lease measure but for the long struggle that undoubtedly lay ahead.[51] In a speech at the dinner of the White House Correspondents' Association on March 15, 1941, four days after he had signed Lend-Lease into law, he revealed in particularly weighty passages something of these innermost feelings.

I remember that, a quarter of a century ago, in the early days of the first World War, the German Government received solemn assurances from their representatives in the United States that the people of America were disunited; that they cared more for peace at any price than for the preservation of ideals and freedom; that there would even be riots and revolutions in the United States if this Nation ever asserted its own interests.

Let not dictators of Europe or Asia doubt our unanimity now ....

Yes, the decisions of our democracy may be slowly arrived at. But when that decision is made, it is proclaimed not with the voice of any one man but with the voice of one hundred and thirty millions. It is binding on us all. And the world is no longer left in doubt.[52]

Administration forces had so deftly organized the passage of the Lend-Lease bill that Roosevelt emerged as the essential victor from the period of debate. A Gallup poll released in mid-April showed his popularity at an all-time high of 73 percent of those with opinions on the subject.[53] The administration was aided by the very active support, among others, of the Committee to Defend America by Aiding the Allies, while the America First Committee worked strenuously in opposition. The CDAAA concentrated its efforts in the Chicago area, the headquarters of America First, and may have been somewhat influential in changing opinions on Lend-Lease in the East Central states, centered around Chicago, where there was a substantial shift from the 39 percent registering in support of the bill in mid-February to the 50 percent supporting it by March 1.[54] The congressional vote, although by and large a partisan one, saw more crossing of party lines than had been the case in the vote for the Neutrality Act of 1939. Passing Lend-Lease by wide margins, Congress in essence gave the President a vote of confidence, which also accurately reflected his overwhelming popular support. The House passed the Lend-Lease measure on February 8, 1941 by a vote of 260 to 165, but when the House took its next vote on March 11, on the issue of accepting the bill as amended by the Senate, the final count was 317 to 71 for acceptance. The Senate passed Lend-Lease on March 8 by a vote of 60 to 31.[55]

The Lend-Lease Act empowered the President, "when he deems it in the interest of national defense," to "authorize the Secretary of War, the Secretary of the Navy, or the head of any other department or agency of the Government . . . to sell, transfer title to, exchange, lease, lend, or otherwise dispose of, to any such government [whose defense the President deemed necessary to the defense of the United States] any defense article." The sweeping powers thus proposed in such legislation were attacked by his opponents during the debate on the bill as tantamount to making Roosevelt a dictator, and a dictator who, worse yet, might very well give away the United States Navy. They contended furthermore, in the most serious allegation of all, that the Lend-Lease Act in essence would mean war for the United States.[56]

When, one year later, the administration sympathizers Davis and Lindley wrote that Lend-Lease "once and for all place[d] this country *in the war* as a nonbelligerent ally of the anti-Axis powers" [emphasis mine],[57] at least two writers were at last coming to terms with the hair-splitting distinction between "nonbelligerency" and being "in the war." To Julius Pratt, the diplomatic historian, Lend-Lease was the time when "the United States entered fully into the condition of nonbelligerency."[58] To be a full nonbelligerent could certainly be regarded as tantamount to being in an undeclared war. Not surprisingly, the administration spokesmen, Hull, Morgenthau, Stimson, Knox, and William Knudsen, who opened the debate with their testimony in congressional committee hearings, avoided any mention of nonbelligerency. Their emphasis was on defense. They spoke only of survival—of the survival of the British navy as necessary to American survival. They pointed out that the American one-ocean navy could then do no more than hold the Japanese off in the Pacific, while the British navy was necessary to protect this hemisphere from a transatlantic invasion. The administration spokesmen talked in no uncertain terms of their belief that, should the British navy be eliminated, an invasion of this hemisphere through South America was a decided possibility. Privately, they acknowledged that even if Lend-Lease were enacted great shipments of materials could not be immediately forthcoming, but the guaranteed prospect of such shipments would bolster British morale, now being sorely tried. Thus, as a morale booster, Lend-Lease might enable Britain to survive the real crisis in the war, which was expected, Stimson and Knox kept emphasizing in the hearings, within sixty to ninety days.[59]

On the other hand, no promises were made, in the opening arguments of administration spokesmen, about avoidance of war. When the opposition, however, began to harp on its theme that Lend-Lease was a measure designed to put America into the war, Roosevelt's response was an emphatic denial. Nothing could be more unequivocal than the following reassurance he gave to Miss Marguerite M. Wells, President of the National League of Women Voters, a week before the enactment of Lend-Lease. "Many thanks for your fine letter of February twenty-eighth." the President wrote on March 4.

I want you to know how deeply I appreciate your clear statement of the position of the League of Women Voters on foreign policy. It is indeed encouraging to know that you and your organization are supporting the

Lease-Lend Bill.

In acknowledging my appreciation of the League's position, I am glad to reiterate the assurance that the policy under which the measure would be operated would not be a war policy but the contrary.[60]

The element of risk that had been stated in the Arsenal of Democracy speech was now no longer alluded to. As the debate over Lend-Lease closed, one must acknowledge that there was serious hedging on that score. A certain degree of unity in the country and a vote of confidence in Congress were achieved at the expense of complete candor.

One of the talking points in the administration's plea for Lend-Lease had been its contention that, in supplying various needy countries, American armaments production would be stepped up. Roosevelt had used this as one of his arguments in the December 17, 1940 press conference in which he had first introduced the idea of Lend-Lease. Secretary of War Stimson had emphasized the point in his testimony during the congressional debate. Then, in his important speech to the White House Correspondents' Association on March 15 Roosevelt called the nation to the task of expanding arms production, saying:

The great task of this day, the deep duty that rests upon each and every one of us is to move products from the assembly lines of our factories to the battle lines of democracy—NOW!

We can have speed, we can have effectiveness, if we maintain our existing unity....

Today, at last—today at long last—ours is not a partial effort. It is a total effort and that is the only way to guarantee ultimate safety.

. . .

Therefore, we are dedicated, from here on, to a constantly increasing tempo of production—a production, greater than we now know or have ever known before—a production that does not stop and should not pause.

... I ask you to consider the needs of our Nation and this hour, to put aside all personal differences until the victory is won.

. . .

And from now on that aid will be increased—and yet again increased—until total victory has been won.[61]

At least one Washington reporter, listening to Roosevelt that Saturday night, heard the muffled drums beat a different message from that which had been sent to Marguerite Wells a week before. "We are all now being carried in the hands of destiny," Raymond Clapper wrote in his column two days later.

... It was strange. It was a war speech without war, a fighting speech without the troops, such a speech as a President might make after war had been declared....

... We see the grave face at the speakers' stand. We hear the voice. ... This is an all-out effort. Nothing short of an all-out effort will win. ... All of our aid. ... From now on that aid will be increased—and yet again increased—until total victory has been won.

Total victory. Fateful words.[62]

6

◊◊◊◊◊◊◊◊◊◊◊◊◊◊◊◊◊◊◊◊◊◊◊◊◊◊◊◊◊◊◊◊◊◊◊◊◊◊◊

THE PRELUDE TO WAR

◊◊◊◊◊◊◊◊◊◊◊◊◊◊◊◊◊◊◊◊◊◊◊◊◊◊◊◊◊◊◊◊◊◊◊◊◊◊◊

The year 1941 was a confusing one. The interventionist segment of the press thought that it saw in the Lend-Lease Act and in Roosevelt's speech to the White House correspondents on March 15 a stage setting for greater American involvement in the war, and began to agitate for United States convoys to Britain.[1] To interventionists at large and to those within his own official family the President appeared to be holding back, to be vacillating and procrastinating, to be failing now to move swiftly enough or in direct enough fashion to the ultimate last stage of total commitment. By the spring of 1941 their impatience with the Rooseveltian leadership, an impatience that had become especially noticeable since the blitzkrieg of 1940,[2] was reaching a crescendo pitch.

Roosevelt had elements other than the interventionists, however, to take into consideration. Isolationists and pacifists were still formidable and continued to be afraid that presidential policies were taking the United States into war. Moreover, while a majority of people, as the polls continued to indicate, felt that United States entrance into the European war was inevitable,[3] they nevertheless shrank from having to face that inevitability. Treading cautiously, in view of these various fears and desires, Roosevelt continued, while slowly involving the United States more and more in the British war effort in the Atlantic, to give ambiguous impressions of the direction in which his foreign policy was going.

91

Although he clearly deemed his purpose, from the post-Munich days onward, must be to render all feasible aid to the Allies, yet to use the word "direction" for Roosevelt's foreign policy is perhaps to employ too strong a term. As his very close aide Tommy "the Cork" Corcoran has maintained, there was no overall plan, no hard and fast adherence to a strategem of any sort. Simply one step at a time was taken, as required by the exigencies of a prevailing situation, and if that step was successful, then one went on to the next.[4] The enactment of Lend-Lease was just such a step, in response to a critical situation, and was a morale booster badly needed by the British as they faced the crisis period in what Churchill named "the Battle of the Atlantic."

The interventionists now expected the momentum to be continued. They had thrilled to Roosevelt's Arsenal of Democracy speech and to his January 6, 1941 State of the Union message to Congress.[5] In the latter he had formally presented the Lend-Lease idea to Congress and had also enunciated the principle of the Four Freedoms, for which, as he saw it, the war was being fought. When, however, for a period of two months after the passage of the Lend-Lease Act Roosevelt made no major address, his interventionist supporters, becoming increasingly uneasy, sought to elicit from him a stronger stance and to prevail upon him to give a much more clearly defined sense of direction.

"For if the trumpet gives an uncertain sound who shall prepare himself for the battle?" wrote the influential Thomas Lamont on May 19, 1941,[6] reflecting the general tone of the communications that were coming to the White House in the late spring of 1941 from agitated internationalists. Roosevelt was being reminded once again that only his voice could effectively speak the necessary words, that only he had the charisma and prestige to give the nation a clear sense of purpose. "Allow me to suggest," wrote one of his correspondents, "that cracker barrel discussions alone as a method of making Americans aware of their peril will get us nowhere. You, our chosen leader, will have to lead us and the increasing peril of the situation demands your leadership. You will have to spell out the peril and tell us blunt truths, in Churchill fashion, about what sacrifices the country must make and what actions it must take."[7] From Cornelius Vanderbilt, Jr. came the following observation:

All over the west I now hear people say "Why doesn't FDR take us more into his confidence? If things are really bad, why doesn't he speak to us more often over the radio?" I think the President ought to make regular fireside chats every 3 or 4 weeks—oftener if necessary. The people are NOT YET FULLY AWAKENED TO THE GRAVITY OF THE SITUATION. They don't know how—or WHY, it may affect them.[8]

There was also pressure from inside his own cabinet. Ickes had long been in favor of a declaration of war.[9] Stimson and Knox had, by the fall of 1940, come to the conclusion that eventually the United States must fight.[10] In mid-May 1941 Morgenthau recorded in his Diary: "I told Hopkins that during the last week or ten days that I had arrived at the conclusion for the first time that if we were going to save England we would have to get into this war."[11] With leading members of Roosevelt's official family agreed upon the inevitablity of United States entry into the war, and with a Gallup poll at the end of April recording 75 percent in favor of United States participation in the war "if it appeared that there was no other way to defeat Germany and Italy," Stimson, who up to the passage of Lend-Lease had felt that the President was both doing and saying all that he possibly could,[12] now grew manifestly impatient with Roosevelt's temporizing. The Secretary of War himself delivered a radio address on May 6, interestingly enough with the prior approval of the President, in which he talked openly of the need for American sacrifice before the conflict in Europe could be ended.[13] On May 24 he wrote Roosevelt asking him to say, at last, the same thing to the American people:

I have been thinking anxiously over the task which confronts you next Tuesday. From what has come to me on all sides I feel certain that the people of the United States are looking to you then to lead and guide them in a situation in which they are now *but anxious to follow you*. Under these circumstances I think it would be disastrous for you to disappoint them. They are not looking for a statement of expedients or halfway measures but for an elucidation of fundamental principles in a grave crisis and, as far as possible, for light on the path which we as a nation must tread to solve that problem.

Stimson then went on to make explicit what he had meant by "the path which we as a nation must tread." Resistance by force would be the only eventual way for America. The American people, he wrote, "must be brought to that momentous resolution by your leadership in explaining why any other course than such forceful resistance would be forever hopeless and abhorrent to every honored principle of American independence and democracy."[14]

Roosevelt had very early, during the spring blitz of 1940 and even

before his cabinet had begun to talk in those terms, privately come
to the conclusion that American entry was unavoidable. But whereas
Stimson felt that the role of a leader was to alert the people to the
necessity of such a course, Roosevelt had another conception of
leadership. A President, Roosevelt felt, could not speak the words
that Stimson was prodding him to say, not if the country were to go
into the long conflict with that degree of unity necessary to weather
it. To his secretary's urgings in the spring of 1941, Roosevelt replied
in the following way: "I know from my experience with Woodrow
Wilson what a terrible thing it is to bring the country into war with
great divisions. I want to have this country as united as it can be if
we go into the war."[15] Possibly Roosevelt was recalling the gist of
Wilson's own remarks to his private secretary Tumulty after the
Lusitania sinking, when Wilson maintained that he could get a
declaration of war if he asked for it but would not go hastily.

When the casualties began to roll in, the people would ask: "Why did Wilson
move so fast in this matter? . . . Why could he not have waited a little longer?"
As the only great nation free to represent peace and sanity, the United States
must hold off until the last possible moment. "When we move against Germany
we must be certain that the whole country not only moves with us but is willing
to go forward to the end with enthusiasm."[16]

After the passage of Lend-Lease, therefore, the President found it
difficult to prepare for his next major speech. He was uncertain just
what he should or could say now to the country. Perhaps for this
reason there was a fair degree of procrastination before the speech.
Scheduled for mid-May, the address was postponed until the end of
the month. Roosevelt gave his speech drafters none of his usual
guidance and up to the last there were frequent changes made in the
text of the speech.[17]

The May 27 address was the first major one since the Arsenal of
Democracy speech, and the President would thus be expected to
make some comment on interim developments in United States
foreign policy. After the passage of Lend-Lease the issue very much
at the forefront of administration thinking, and of isolationist fears,
was that of convoying. From the beginning of 1941 Hitler had
stepped up the war at sea, and British shipping losses were mounting.
A British Admiralty report disclosing that 115,000 tons of Allied
shipping had been destroyed in less than two months was forwarded
by Churchill to Roosevelt on March 20, 1941.[18] Once Lend-Lease
was enacted, therefore, the question of how to insure the delivery of

American materials was very much the main question of the day. United States Navy convoys would be an answer, but convoying was distinctly a wartime practice, associated in the public mind with American participation in World War I. It was not a word that could be mentioned without conjuring up the specter of United States entry into this second world war. Senator Burton K. Wheeler explicitly stated the thought in many minds when he declared in early April: "I realized from the first, after the Lend-Lease bill was passed, that the next step would be that the warmongers in this country would cry for convoys, and everyone recognizes the fact that convoys mean war."[19]

Still the pressure was great to do something to mitigate shipping losses. In the month of April Roosevelt had first approved Hemisphere Defense Plan No. 1, which sanctioned aggressive action by the navy against German submarines in the Western Atlantic, but then had rescinded the order, thus holding back from any thing that smacked of convoying. On the other hand, he soon took a definite step toward widening American action in the Atlantic by authorizing naval patrols beyond the 300-mile neutrality belt which had been proclaimed in the early days of the war. Patrols were now to go as far as halfway across the Atlantic, to longitude 25°. The American navy, although still forbidden to shoot at German submarines in the area, could at least inform the British of their presence.[20] Cautious about public opinion, Roosevelt, when cabling Churchill on the extension of the Atlantic patrol, added: "It is not certain that I would make a specific announcement. I may decide to issue the necessary naval operative orders and let time bring out the existence of the new patrol area."[21]

Soon members of the administration and then Roosevelt himself in a press conference talked, albeit with a certain amount of evasion, about the extended patrol. Then in the May 27 speech the President spoke to the country of the new actions in the Atlantic, but in such a way as to relate them most particularly to defense of the Western Hemisphere:

> The Azores and the Cape Verde Islands, if occupied or controlled by Germany, would directly endanger the freedom of the Atlantic and our own American physical safety. . . . They would provide a springboard for actual attack against the integrity and the independence of Brazil and her neighboring Republics.
>
> • • •
>
> Anyone with an atlas, anyone with a reasonable knowledge of the sudden striking force of modern war, knows that it is stupid to wait until a probable

enemy has gained a foothold from which to attack. Old-fashioned common sense calls for the use of a strategy that will prevent such an enemy from gaining a foothold in the first place.

We have, accordingly, extended our patrol in North and South Atlantic waters. We are steadily adding more and more ships and planes to that patrol. It is well known that the strength of the Atlantic Fleet has been greatly increased during the past year [Roosevelt had recently ordered three battleships, an aircraft carrier, and supporting ships to be transferred from the Pacific Fleet stationed at Pearl Harbor to the Atlantic], and that it is constantly being built up.

These ships and planes warn of the presence of attacking raiders, on the sea, under the sea, and above the sea. The danger from these raiders is, of course, greatly lessened if their location is definitely known. We are thus being forewarned. We shall be on our guard against efforts to establish Nazi bases closer to our hemisphere.

In another portion of the speech, however, and in a somewhat surreptitious manner, Roosevelt disclosed the primary reason for the patrol:

... from the point of view of strict naval and military necessity, we shall give every possible assistance to Britain and to all who, with Britain, are resisting Hitlerism or its equivalent with force of arms. Our patrols are helping now to insure delivery of the needed supplies to Britain.

From here he went on to an even stronger pledge:

All additional measures necessary to deliver the goods will be taken. Any and all further methods or combination of methods, which can or should be utilized, are being devised by our military and naval technicians, who, with me, will work out and put into effect such new and additional safeguards as may be needed.

I say that the delivery of needed supplies to Britain is imperative. I say that this can be done; it must be done, and it will be done.

In a sense, to "insure delivery of the needed supplies to Britain" could be construed as a means to defend the Western Hemisphere by keeping Britain alive and in the war. But this was defense at a distance, rather than the point Roosevelt had made earlier in the speech when he had spoken of precluding a direct and immediate attack on the Western Hemisphere.

Roosevelt ended his address with the declaration of an unlimited national emergency:

Therefore, with profound consciousness of my responsibilities to my country-men and to my country's cause, I have tonight issued a proclamation that an unlimited national emergency exists and requires the strengthening of our defense to the extreme limit of our national power and authority.

The Nation will expect all individuals and all groups to play their full parts, without stint, and without selfishness, and without doubt that our democracy will triumphantly survive.[22]

"Unlimited national emergency" was indeed a strong statement, and Roosevelt's decision to include it was not made until just a few days before the speech.[23] Certain other parts of the speech contained forceful language. The President had even gone so far as to explicitly disclose the gravity of the situation on the high seas, saying:

The blunt truth is this—and I reveal this with full knowledge of the British Government: the present rate of Nazi sinkings of merchant ships is more than three times as high as the capacity of British shipyards to replace them; it is more than twice the combined British and American output of merchant ships today.

But the rhetoric was stronger than the actual intent of the speech, and even the words, Stimson noted in his Diary, had been "softened down" by Roosevelt in delivery.[24] The following day, when meeting with the press, Roosevelt, to the great disappointment of the interventionists, injected a note of ambiguity by indicating that he had no immediate intention of following up his declaration of an unlimited national emergency with specific proposals. The night before he had been heartened by the good response which the speech had gotten in the country. Commenting to Sherwood on the many telegrams he had just received, he had been amazed to find them "ninety-five per cent favorable" and added, "And I figured I'd be lucky to get an even break on this speech."[25] Now, rather than take another giant step by implementing the declaration of an unlimited national emergency, he was simply content to let things rest as they were.

His objective all along had been to carry the country with him. Having once more strengthened the confidence of the majority, he now had no wish to antagonize the minority of strong isolationists, whose support he and the country would ultimately need at the time of American entrance into the war. His tactic was to keep with him those whose support he had now gained and to take no overly provocative step that would only irrevocably alienate those whose support he still hoped to gain. Therefore, when he was asked to be specific about the meaning of "unlimited national emergency," he backed away, perhaps feeling that exact definitions would be

politically unwise and serve only to lose groups that might come to
him in the future.[26] As a close associate later put it, FDR, always
conscious of the whole country, held that as the head of a nation he
would be more effective if he hadn't crossed the Rubicon.[27]

Consequently, he chose not to act upon the declaration of
unlimited national emergency, which he had made possibly only to
have it available for future use.[28] Without concrete follow-up steps
the overall effect of the address was one of vagueness. General Wood,
chairman of the America First Committee, summed it up when he
called the May 27 address "the least war-like of any of [Roosevelt's]
utterances since election."[29] James Twohey, an analyzer of trends in
press opinion, noted a few months later:

Mr. Roosevelt's fireside speeches have almost always attempted to point up and
crystallize opinion in positive support of some definite objective, but this
speech, while it rallied opinion in momentary unity behind the President, did not
seem to precipitate support of any one positive course. It merely seemed to mean
all things to the press.[30]

Since there was no one measure, such as Lend-Lease, to rally the
country to support, and since Roosevelt's guiding objective, as far as
public opinion was concerned, was simply to keep it with him, the
vagueness of the speech and the remarks in the subsequent press
conference fitted the purpose admirably. A week later Roosevelt was
still congratulating himself on the way things had turned out, when
he wrote his good friends in England Faith and Arthur Murray:

It has been possible, as you know, for me to carry the country along slowly, but
I think surely, and last week's speech met with far more approval—I should guess
at least seventy-five or eighty per cent—than if I had given it even two weeks
before.[31]

In the letter to the Murrays Roosevelt touched upon two things in
which he took special pride—his intuitive sense of public feeling and
his sure sense of timing. Early in May he had been especially wary of
the stir being made by the interventionists. It was at that time that
Roosevelt had postponed his scheduled May address to the end of
the month, pleading a persistent cold. "What he's suffering from
most of all," Missy LeHand informed Robert Sherwood, "is a case of
sheer exasperation."[32] Public opinion polls released in May had
shown a strong downward trend in public sentiment in favor of aid
to Britain even at the risk of war,[33] and Roosevelt had apparently

felt that the time was not right for him to frighten the people unduly with an advanced interventionist position. According to Twohey's analysis of press opinion, this is exactly what the press had been doing in the six or seven weeks since the passage of the Lend-Lease Act. Twohey found the press at this time overwhelmingly interventionist, and within that interventionist press an overwhelmingly high majority of newspapers were demanding that the U.S. convoy goods to Britain. Roosevelt's fireside speech of May 27, according to the Twohey interpretation, was intended as a deflationary measure to counteract the war hysteria that the press had raised in the interventionist camp.[34]

If it was Roosevelt's purpose in the speech to calm the public while at the same time "to carry the country along slowly, but I think surely," he succeeded admirably well. By June 14 the Gallup poll showed a jump to 55 percent in favor of convoying, whereas the percentages had been 41 percent in an April poll and consistently 52 percent in two May polls.[35]

With Hitler's invasion of Russia on June 22, and Russia's entry into the war on the side of the Allies, major attention shifted to the question of aid to Russia. The Gallup poll showed that the American people, still distrustful of communism, did not favor sending aid to Russia on the same basis as it was being given to Britain.[36] At first not certain that Russia could hold out, Roosevelt very soon began to think that she would survive the German summer drive, and slowly in July, without public announcement, the administration made plans to send her aid. In August, when the announcement of the aid program was made, the American people, by that time impressed with Soviet resistance, reacted favorably.[37]

The other persistently nagging and persistently unresolved question of the summer was when, at last, to go to convoying. After the United States occupied Iceland in early July, Roosevelt approved Hemisphere Defense Plan IV, which provided for convoys to Iceland and also allowed ships of other than United States nationality to join the United States convoys. Accordingly, British ships transporting lend-lease supplies to England would be protected along the greater part of the North Atlantic route. But before the orders could be acted upon, Roosevelt, worried over public opinion, rescinded that part which enabled other ships to combine with Unites States convoys. With United States public opinion on convoying hovering around the 55 percent mark, Roosevelt hesitated in the summer of 1941 to take that necessary, but unpopular, step.[38]

It was during the somewhat quieter period of the summer months, when there was less goading from the interventionist press,[39] that Roosevelt again encouraged the activities of the prodders. Convoying could be put off only so long, the question of renewal of the Selective Service Act of 1940 was in the offing, and repeal of the last restrictions in the Neutrality Act would eventually have to be considered. As in the summer of 1940 Roosevelt again needed help from articulate public figures to create the right climate of opinion in which these steps could be taken. A most advanced interventionist group, the Fight for Freedom Committee, had been organized in April 1941. The chairman of its executive committee, Ulric Bell, had long had close relations with members of the White House staff and had acted as liaison between the government and the more informal Century Group, in existence since the summer of 1940 and out of which the Fight for Freedom Committee had evolved. When, at one point during the summer of 1941, Ulric Bell thought it best to check with the White House before his committee published a particularly harsh indictment of administration shilly-shallying, Roosevelt surprised his visitor by suggesting, "If you're going to give me hell, why not use some really strong language?" With his penchant for seeking out the most direct phrase, Roosevelt added, "You know, 'pusillanimous' isn't such a bad word."[40]

White House files reveal that Roosevelt's office staff made a concerted effort to line up speakers advocating advanced policy positions. Sometimes this was done in connection with the Fight for Freedom Committee. The following urgent telegram request, sent on June 16 to Steve Early by Robert Sherwood, reveals much about the activity of the White House staffers:

Dear Steve: There is to be a great negro mass meeting in Harlem at two thirty next Sunday afternoon under the auspices of the Fight for Freedom Committee. I have agreed to speak and so has Dorothy Parker and some negro leaders, but they are desperate to get some real star attraction.

Would there be any chance of persuading Senator Meade [*sic*] to speak? The main speech will be broadcast at least locally. If not Meade, could you suggest anyone else from the Administration?

I apologize for bothering you, but Harlem has been deluged with hostile propaganda [in his book *Roosevelt and Hopkins* Sherwood explains, "The Communists were very active among the Negro population in these days and since."][41] and this is a fine chance to counteract it. My address is 25 Sutton Place, New York City. Very best regards.

Bob Sherwood

Early answered two days later:

Finally reached Meade. He scheduled speak Utica Saturday and deliver two addresses Sunday in Western New York. Therefore, suggest Ulric Bell telephone Senator Josh Lee, Oklahoma, who is excellent speaker and "all out." Also am trying Senator Pepper.   He away but returns Washington late today. Regards.[42]

In the crucial summer of 1940 Roosevelt had had a very special relationship with the White Committee. Now, in the summer and fall of 1941 his staff maintained a close working relationship with the Fight for Freedom Committee. How close their association was is suggested by the following pieces in the Roosevelt files. A telegram to Roosevelt from Ulric Bell, dated November 24, 1941, reads as follows: "Justice Douglas is considering addressing American Youth for Freedom Fighting Rally here Nov. 11th and we believe his participation would have profound effect at this time. Barry Bingham suggests I ask you to use your good offices. Felicitations." The following day the President's secretary, Marvin McIntyre, turned the telegram over to Lowell Mellett, a Roosevelt aide, accompanied by the following memorandum: "Since you have been guilty before where the 'elect' are concerned, will you handle this and acknowledge to Ulric?"[43]

As the United States inched closer to war, the isolationists became more strident in their attacks on administration policy. Isolationist sentiment and activity both in and out of Congress presented a formidable damper to further administration actions.[44] The seriousness with which this problem was regarded is evident in the long and detailed report requested by Steve Early on radio time given to isolationist and interventionist speakers from January 1, 1941 to October 31, 1941. The report included a breakdown of those speaking as individuals and those speaking under the auspices of committees. It also included breakdowns by network and a chronological listing of all speeches. The interventionists came out slightly ahead, with a national network time of 72 hours, 56 minutes as opposed to 62 hours, 32 minutes for the isolationists.[45]

As the fall wore on the administration sought speakers for its side with an increasing sense of urgency. Barry Bingham, publisher of the *Louisville Courier-Journal*, had organized a Speaker's Bureau within the Democratic National Committee. When Bingham sent a letter to the President asking for aid in getting the Vice President, Senator Barkley, and several other senators to talk on behalf of the administration's side of foreign policy before large public meetings and on radio broadcasts, Roosevelt responded immediately by forwarding the request to Vice President Wallace. Wallace offered to speak once a month, and suggested certain senators who might aid in drawing up a roster of speakers. Roosevelt found "the suggestion . . . grand that you make one important speech a month," and acknowledged that he was "sending word to Barry Bingham to work with the Senators you mentioned."[46] Although the administration's effort to secure spokesmen was a sizable one, the response from congressmen was disheartening, as evidenced in the following letter from Archibald MacLeish, Director of the Office of Facts and Figures:[47]

At the meeting of the National Executive Committee of the Committee to Defend America and Fight for Freedom, there was apparently a lengthy discussion of the difficulty experienced, even with the cooperation of Mr. Barry Bingham's excellent Speaker's Bureau, in securing speakers ready to speak on behalf of the Administration's policy throughout the country. Senators Pepper and Lee, and particularly Senator Pepper, have carried most of the load. It is an understandable feeling that we ought somehow to increase the size of the roster of administrative spokesmen available.[48]

In view of the problems the White House had been experiencing that fall in getting support both in and out of Congress for what it had considered the very minimum in necessary legislation, it is understandable that its friends should have been concerned with "increasing the size of the roster of administrative spokesmen." The extension of Selective Service is a case in point. The first peacetime draft in United States history, calling for induction of draftees for a one-year period, had been enacted by Congress in September 1940. Potentially an explosive issue, the Selective Service Act of 1940 had been made palatable at the time to the public and the Congress by two factors: it had been considered in the period immediately following the fall of France, and the Republican candidate for the presidency, Wendell Willkie, had endorsed it, thus making it a non-political issue. But when the administration sought to extend the act in 1941, it met serious difficulties, some of which were of its own making. Succumbing to the urgings of Secretaries Stimson and Knox and the Army Chief of Staff, General George C. Marshall, Roosevelt allowed resolutions to be introduced sanctioning the stationing of draftees outside the Western Hemisphere and calling for an indefinite extension of service time for the duration of the national emergency. Congress refused the former and allowed only an eighteen-month extension period. Even with these alterations of the resolutions, the Senate extended the act by a vote of only 45 to 30, while the House passed the measure on August 12 by only a one-vote margin, 203-202.[49]

There are plausible explanations for the closeness of the vote. First, it is likely that isolationist sentiment in Congress exceeded that of the public at large. Secondly, congressmen are always exceptionally wary of the critical minority element in their constituency and anxious not to give offense to this group, which is watching them closely and is much quicker to voice its displeasure than the affirmative majority is to express its feelings.[50] Roosevelt supporters, however, although undoubtedly aware of the political considerations that govern congressional voting, were shocked by the one-vote margin. It made such an impression that even today this vote is cited most frequently by those who lived through this period to indicate the surprising strength of isolationism as late as the fall of 1941.[51]

Thus it is understandable why Roosevelt vacillated for so long on the convoy issue. Finally he seized upon an incident in the Atlantic involving a German submarine and the American destroyer *Greer* to announce his decision to authorize convoying. In a fighting speech on September 11, mentioning other incidents as well as that of the *Greer*, Roosevelt branded German submarines as "rattlesnakes of the Atlantic." He asserted that America's answer would be "very simply, very clearly, that our patrolling vessels and planes will protect all merchant ships—not only American ships but ships of any flag —engaged in commerce in our defensive waters."[52]

Then, in his strongest speech before Pearl Harbor, the Navy Day speech of October 27, 1941, Roosevelt underscored his persistent warnings to the American people that Hitler constituted a real threat to their national security by now speaking of two documents in the possession of the United States government. The first was "a secret map made in Germany . . . of South America and a part of Central America," dividing that area, including Panama, into "five vassal states, bringing the whole continent under their domination." Secondly, Roosevelt reported, "Your Government has in its possession another document. . . . It is a detailed plan . . . to abolish all religions" in the world areas dominated by the Reich, and to "set up an International Nazi Church." The implications were that if these things happened the American way of life could not continue, and that the strategic threat to the Panama Canal itself was alone enough to threaten the independence of the United States. In this same speech Roosevelt utilized another incident in the Atlantic in order to make the assertion.

> We have wished to avoid shooting. But the shooting has started. And history has recorded who fired the first shot. In the long run, however, all that will matter is who fired the last shot.
>   America has been attacked. The U.S.S. *Kearny* is not just a Navy ship. She belongs to every man, women, and child in this Nation.
>
>   • • •
>
>   Today in the face of this newest and greatest challenge . . . we Americans have cleared our decks and taken our battle stations. We stand ready in the defense of our Nation and in the faith of our fathers to do what God has given us the power to see as our full duty.[53]

The speech carried the intimation that it was now only a matter of time before the United States entered a declared war and acknowledged that it was already in an undeclared war. But Congress remained reluctant to go nearer to the final eventuality. Although it revised the Neutrality Act in November to provide for the arming of merchant ships and to allow their sailing into belligerent ports, the vote to do so was by a narrow margin.[54] Armed merchant ships would only create more naval incidents, which ultimately would offer provocation enough for a declaration of war.

Roosevelt had barely gotten legislation supporting his foreign policy in the last half of 1941. He had not been rebuffed, however, though the vote was precariously close on the extension of Selective Service. He had brought the country into an undeclared naval war, while providing for the retention of a trained fighting force. The months since the passage of Lend-Lease had been the most difficult ones of all and had required all Roosevelt's skill in navigating the choppy seas of public opinion in order to urge minimum necessary steps on a reluctant country and still preserve its confidence in the ultimate wisdom of his leadership.

7

THE HELMSMAN'S SKILL

"No statesman in the world saw and described the Nazi menace more truly than Franklin Roosevelt," Stimson recorded in his memoirs.[1] And one might add that the President was earlier than most to see the threat. With a penetrating intelligence and a background and penchant for foreign affairs, Roosevelt was a President admirably equipped for the handling of foreign policy. But in the early thirties, weighted down with problems of the depression, and living in a time of irresolute leadership and a certain loss of nerve in the Western European democracies, Roosevelt had exerted himself only spasmodically to try to stem the tide of aggression in Europe. At home, he had coped as best he could with an isolationist public, whose hatred of war he had shared without entirely sharing its conviction that the neutrality legislation of 1935-1937 would keep this country out of war.

With the Quarantine speech of 1937 he had made an effort to reverse America's isolationist outlook. But then, feeling that reaction to the speech was too vigorously unfavorable, he had henceforth hesitated to take a strong position in advance of public opinion. Although there were many times after the outbreak of World War II in Europe that Roosevelt had used forceful rhetoric in denunciation of Hitler, he had presented his programs to the nation in such a way as to minimize the risk of war that they involved, emphasizing rather that they were steps in the direction of peace. At the same time, from the post-Munich days onward, moving with a sense of direction that he had lacked before, Roosevelt had taken each necessary step, as he saw it, and in so doing had involved the country more and more in the war effort, bringing it closer and closer to its ultimate entrance as a fully participating ally.

One of these steps had been the extension of the American patrol to the mid-Atlantic in the spring of 1941. As U.S. activity increased on the high seas, "incidents" with German submarines were bound to occur. Inevitably there was speculation about the administration's deliberate courting of incidents. When reporting, in June 1941, on the involvement of an American destroyer with a German submarine, the Washington columnists Alsop and Kintner had gone so far as to contend that it was Roosevelt's hope that the Atlantic patrol would produce just such an encounter "to serve as the pretext for really strong action by this country."[2]

Of course it was known that incidents would develop as American activities in the Atlantic were extended; Roosevelt was not averse to using such incidents to justify stronger and stronger measures, the most striking example of which is the use of the *Greer* episode at the end of the summer to announce the policy of convoying. Yet to suppose that it was the administration's deliberate purpose to create incidents in order to get into the war is to give a greatly oversimplified explanation of what was actually taking place in 1941. Of course Roosevelt knew that the United States would eventually have to go to war. He had suspected it with the outbreak of world war in 1939 and had accepted it, after the blitzkrieg of 1940, as the only way to defeat Hitler. But what he was doing from the summer of 1940 to the fall of 1941 was simply taking the steps he thought necessary to keep Britain in the war, to keep the British navy afloat, and to protect British supply lines. His primary concern was to keep those supply lines open. Even so, he hesitated for a long time to do all that was necessary (convoying, for instance) for fear of an adverse reaction from the American public. And even when he went to convoying he did so with the realization that Hitler would not wish to use this as a provocation for war while he was still in the midst of his Russian campaign.[3]

Roosevelt worked within the ambivalences that face a democratic leader, who can never hope to be full master of his own foreign policy, but who must wait on public opinion and the inexorable march of events, knowing all the while that essentially the initiative in foreign policy making does not lie with him. He can never have the kind of control that totalitarian leadership has. His role is, more often than not, to react to developments from overseas. This is the unwritten rule which democratic leaders flout at their peril. An unabashedly bellicose foreign policy foisted upon what is at most times an essentially peace-loving people will eventually backfire, tearing the country apart, and calling into suspicion that leader who has misjudged the intrinsic restraints on leadership in a democracy and who has thereby overstepped his mandate.

While presidential conduct was of necessity circumscribed, American and British military staffs went ahead to work out a blueprint for action predicated on America's entrance into the war. From January 29 to March 29, 1941 they held secret, unprecedented conversations in Washington, out of which emerged the plan ABC-1. ABC-1 had grown out of an earlier American version, Plan Dog, which had been contained in a memorandum sent to the President on November 12, 1940 by Admiral Stark, Chief of Naval Operations. Army Chief of Staff General Marshall and Secretary of War Stimson had concurred with the ideas of the Stark memorandum, which called for a strategy, in the event the United States became involved in war with the Tripartite Pact powers, to be based on a concentrated effort first against Hitler and a holding action in the Pacific until the European war had been attended to. While neither approving nor disapproving of Plan Dog, Roosevelt had agreed to authorize the 1941 joint staff talks when pressured by his military advisers, and in particular by the navy men on both sides of the Atlantic, Admiral Stark here and Stark's counterpart in London, Admiral Pound. Although it was emphasized by the Americans to their British guests that these were solely military talks and in no way binding upon the political leadership, ABC-1 certainly made for closer cooperation with the British, so close that Robert Sherwood has termed this prewar understanding the "common-law alliance."[4]

Thus the grand strategy of the war was worked out months prior to America's entry, and in the remaining months of 1941 the United States concentrated its efforts on making the Atlantic sector more secure. When Roosevelt met Churchill at the Atlantic Conference in August he talked of his hope that he could "baby Japan along" for three months while the United States directed all attention to supplying the British, and to a lesser extent the Russians and Chinese.[5] And as the administration took more and more action to keep the Atlantic supply lines open, the isolationists became more critical of America's increasing involvement in the Atlantic war. But the interventionists themselves were far from happy with the supply situation and roundly assailed the government for dragging its feet in one vitally important area—war production.

During the precarious days of the 1940 blitz Roosevelt had first attempted to deal with the production problem by establishing the Advisory Commission to the Council of National Defense (NDAC), a body which had proved ineffective for several reasons, one of which was its purely advisory character and the most obvious of which was the fact that it lacked a central coordinator. By the end of that year, when Lend-Lease was being proposed, the question of production took on a new urgency. Just three days after he had first presented the idea of Lend-Lease in his press conference of December 17, 1940, Roosevelt announced in a special press conference on December 20 that he was setting up the Office of Production Management (OPM) within the Office of Emergency Management of the Executive Office of the President. The NDAC was still being retained, but the OPM was now created in an effort "to simplify and concentrate responsibility."[6] The OPM was given broad powers to

increase, accelerate, and regulate the production and supply of materials, articles, and equipment and the provision of emergency plant facilities and services required for the national defense, and to insure . . . coordination of those activities of the several departments, corporations, and other agencies of the Government which are directly concerned therewith.[7]

It was jointly headed by Knudsen and Hillman, members of the NDAC, who had represented business and labor on that commission. Roosevelt was still resisting the plan that Bernard Baruch, chairman of the World War I War Industries Board, had long been advocating —a production agency under one man serving in the capacity of economic czar.

Continuing to improvise, Roosevelt in April 1941 created the Office of Price Administration and Civilian Supply headed by Leon Henderson, also a member of the Advisory Commission. As Judge Rosenman explains, OPA was to take over "the functions of the commissioners on price stabilization and consumer protection of the National Defense Advisory Commission. This left the NDAC with functions relating only to agriculture and transportation."[8] As the OPM and OPA became involved in disputes on allocations of supplies between military and consumer needs, a new agency was brought into being in August 1941, the Supply Priorities and Allocation

Board (SPAB). SPAB's membership was made up of Knudsen, Hillman, Henderson, and Harry Hopkins (who as Special Assistant to the President was supervising the Lend-Lease program); its executive director was Donald M. Nelson of Sears, Roebuck, and its chairman was Vice President Wallace.[9]

By the end of 1941, therefore, the NDAC was being phased out and a proliferation of new agencies had been created in its stead. It was not until January 1942 that Roosevelt organized the sort of agency envisioned by Baruch, the War Production Board, which Baruch would have liked to have been asked to head, but which was placed under Donald Nelson.[10] Nelson proved not forceful enough for the task of economic czar, and after a time the needed effective coordinator of war production was found when Justice James F. Byrnes, under a series of titles, came to assume that role.

In spite of the fact that industrial conditions in the eighteen-month "defense" period preceding Pearl Harbor were quite chaotic, production of war materials was increasing substantially.[11] Nevertheless Roosevelt was under a great deal of criticism for the slowness of the tempo, which was mainly attributed to the fact that he had not vested authority in one man. The problem, however, was much more than the absence of a single effective director. Langer and Gleason explicitly define the difficulty of the "defense period" when they speak of "the virtual impossibility of fully rearming a democratic nation in the absence of the psychology begotten of actual war."[12] Industrialists, still tied to a depression philosophy of an economy of scarcity, were fearful of overexpansion and hesitated to convert to large-scale war production for an emergency the length of which was still a great uncertainty. Labor, fresh from the hours and wages gains of the New Deal, resisted the thought of any extension of the forty-hour week at the same rate of pay. The consumer, with a "guns and butter" attitude, expected no lowering of the civilian standard of living, and industry complied in the year 1941 by actually producing automobiles at the highest peak since 1929.[13]

In the blitz days of 1940, when he had been trying to calm a jittery nation, Roosevelt had even lent himself to the encouragement of this kind of consumer mentality. In his press conference of May 28, 1940, commenting on the good response to his fireside chat two days earlier on national defense, he had said:

In other words, the answer has been fine all over the country, I am very, very appreciative of it and I think people understand the seriousness of the situation.

Then he had added:

At the same time, I think people should realize that we are not going to upset, any more than we have to, a great many of the normal processes of life. There is one of the ladies in the room, for instance, who was going to ask that question, and wanted to know whether we are not only going to have no new automobiles next year, new models, but whether it means a lot of other things that could be put into the luxury class would have to be foregone by the population ... the answer is that this delightful young lady will not have to forego cosmetics, lipsticks, ice-cream sodas–(*Laughter*)[14]

One of his appointees to the NDAC that month was an adviser on consumer protection, Miss Harriet Elliott, Dean of Women at the University of North Carolina. When Frances Perkins, the Secretary of Labor, had objected to this appointment, Roosevelt explained the rationale in back of it was that "we have to have a woman. Got to pacify the women. If there is a woman, you won't have women's protests against actions that are too military, against giving too much help to the allies. The presence of a woman on the Commission will stop all that."[15]

In that panicky May of 1940, when Roosevelt must have been very much concerned with not "scaring the American people into thinking they are going to be dragged into this war,"[16] the emphasis had been on reassurance. His fireside speech to the nation on May 26, 1940 had attempted to convey, along with a sense of urgency, a sense of confidence. "Let us not be calamity-howlers and discount our strength," he had pleaded. "Let us calmly consider what we have done and what we must do." While "calling upon the resources, the efficiency and the ingenuity of the American manufacturers of war material of all kinds," he had pledged that he would not allow the emergency to be used as an excuse for scrapping the economic and social gains of the New Deal, asserting that "there is nothing in our present emergency to justify a retreat from any of our social objectives."[17]

This kind of reassurance had been needed in the bleak summer of 1940. Roosevelt knew his countrymen well and sensed how near to panic they could come at the thought that America was approaching full participation in the war. Robert Sherwood, who by the fall was helping to write the President's campaign speeches, acknowledges that when Wendell Willkie raised the war issue during the campaign, he (Sherwood) "was amazed and horrified at the evidences of hysteria. . . . The fear of war was . . . something new and unreasoning and tending toward a sense of panic. . . . it was difficult to avoid the dismaying thought that perhaps the American people were ready to stampede along the road which led to Bordeaux and so to Vichy even before the Panzers arrived on our home soil."[18]

By the following year, when Lend-Lease had been enacted and production requirements were all the more pressing, Roosevelt was saying to the American people something quite different from his message of May 1940. In the speech of March 15, 1941, four days after he had signed Lend-Lease into law, he stated:

We shall have to make sacrifices—every one of us. The final extent of those sacrifices will depend on the speed with which we act NOW!

Whether you are in the armed services; whether you are a steelworker or a stevedore; a machinist or a housewife; a farmer or a banker; a storekeeper or a manufacturer—to all of you it will mean sacrifice in behalf of your country and your liberties. Yes, you will feel the impact of this gigantic effort in your daily lives. You will feel it in a way that will cause, to you, many inconveniences.

• • •

A halfhearted effort on our part will lead to failure. This is no part-time job. The concepts of "business as usual," of "normalcy," must be forgotten until the task is finished. Yes, it's an all-out effort—and nothing short of an all-out effort will win.[19]

Yet the total effort was not made. Industrialists did not put war production into full gear and the plants that were engaged were plagued by a rash of strikes, beginning in January 1941, in part but not entirely caused by communist agitators bent on sabotaging war production. One of the strongest criticisms raised by its friends against the administration that year was the charge that it was lax in dealing with the strike situation. But Roosevelt, always conscious of the self-imposed restraints within which a democratic government must operate if it were not to flout the very meaning of the word democracy, hesitated to take coercive action against the strikers. Force might bring a hardening of public attitude against the government itself. More than this, coercion was something that a democracy resorted to at its own peril. Roosevelt's feeling that strong-arm tactics were unconscionable in a republic is nowhere better illustrated than in the remark he had once made to Rexford Tugwell, an original brain truster and a future Roosevelt biographer, to the effect that General Douglas MacArthur, who had driven the 1932 Bonus Army of veterans from Washington's Anacostia Flats, was "one of the two most dangerous men in the country."[20] And Robert Sherwood reports that when the North American Aviation

Plant at Inglewood, California was seriously disrupted by a communist-led strike and the President felt compelled, on June 9, 1941, "for the first time in his career to order armed intervention by the U.S. Army," the "decision . . . was deeply repugnant to him."[21]

Critics bewailed what appeared to be Roosevelt's lackadaisical attitude toward war production, but his grasp of the magnitude of the effort which would soon have to come dictated the careful way in which he was preparing the country to respond with total dedication. By consciously doing nothing in 1941 to intensify divisions within the American populace he was in a positive sense readying the nation to make the unified drive, once America was fully in the war, that was essential for victory. He had a great faith in the dynamic quality and potential of American industry. Fifty thousand planes a year had seemed to him believable in 1940, before others thought it possible. Clinton Rossiter, expressing a sentiment which most historians would echo, talks of Roosevelt's "breadth of vision, which in time of war gave him a clearer grasp of America's productive potential than the leaders of industry seemed to have themselves."[22] But when Roosevelt referred, in June 1941, to "the mass production which must come in the year ahead,"[23] he knew that that production would only come if the American people had been properly prepared to make the gigantic response of which they were capable.

*   *   *

As is now evident to us, Roosevelt saw earlier than most the whole shape of things to come, grasping the direction in which the inexorable march of events was taking the country. Donald Nelson later reminisced:

But let's think back to that June of 1940: Who among us, except the President of the United States, really saw the magnitude of the job ahead, the awful mission of the United States in a world running berserk? . . . None of us — not one that I know of, except the President—saw that we might be fighting Germany and Japan all over the world.[24]

Frances Perkins sees in the creation of the NDAC in May 1940 an indication that he was thinking of American entrance into the war and gearing himself for that eventuality.[25] Judge Rosenman's conviction that Roosevelt had accepted the idea of American entry since the blitz days of 1940 has already been noted.

When Roosevelt continued, however, to be circumspect in his public statements, interventionist impatience with him began to be openly noticeable. By mid-summer of 1940 Bernard De Voto was observing to Elmer Davis, "All the commentators have been saying that, for the first time, Roosevelt is behind public sentiment in the matter of armaments and aggression."[26]

As some members of his cabinet began to catch up to him in the thought that war was inevitable, they also registered complaints about his leadership. Ickes, who had long thought that the President's statements and actions should have been more forceful than they were, wrote in his Diary in the spring of 1941:

I do know that in every direction I find a growing discontent with the President's lack of leadership. He still has the country if he will take it and lead it. But he won't have it much longer unless he does something. It won't be sufficient for him to make another speech and then go into a state of innocuous desuetude again. People are beginning to say: "I am tired of words; I want action."[27]

Stimson in that same spring prodded Roosevelt to present the case for a declaration of war to the American people. The Secretary of War felt that the time was right for such a step because of poll indications that nearly three-fourths of the people were willing to go to war *if* that were the only way to defeat Germany. Since it was being conceded within the administration that this was the only means by which Hitler could be defeated, Roosevelt ought now to say this, Stimson argued, to the American people. When Roosevelt refused to do so, but chose rather to wait for events to impress themselves upon the people, Stimson felt that the President was failing in his "duty to lead."[28] Stimson's biographer reports that the Secretary "was forced to believe that in the crisis of 1941 T.R. would have done a better and more clean-cut job than was actually done. . . . T.R.'s advantage would have been in his natural boldness, his firm conviction that where he led, men would follow. He would . . . have been able to brush aside the contemptible little group of men who wailed of 'warmongers,' and in the blunt strokes of a poster painter he would have demonstrated the duty of Americans in a world issue."[29]

Political scientists have tended to agree with the Stimsonian view of leadership. Usually they have advocated for the presidency that it be an office of authority and have been happiest with Presidents who have come closest to approximating the role of the British Prime Minister. They have thought government works best where there is a clear-cut sense of direction, and that this can come most easily from the presidential office. Thus they, like Stimson, have tended to pass rather harsh judgment on Roosevelt's temporizing in the months before Pearl Harbor.

But Roosevelt had his own sense of what leadership should be, the sense of a man whose life experience had been with the practical aspects of politics. The man who prided himself on being a "realist" understood what so often the theorists fail to take into account as they fashion their blueprints. He knew that this was a country of disparate groupings, whose very fears and prejudices were being intensified by the appeals of such leading isolationist spokesmen as Charles A. Lindbergh. He realized, too, that such disunity had to be overcome if the effort required in a total war was ever to be made. Resolution was essential to the large task ahead. Therefore, Roosevelt moved slowly, consciously giving the nation time to make up its mind, hoping it would be educated by events, and hoping also by his stopping short of the clarion call that the underlying disunities in this society would be ameliorated rather than intensified.

The true test of a democratic leader, as Franklin Roosevelt understood it, was to preserve the vital aspects of democracy even in the midst of the emergency situation then at hand. The very fact that in this period of history not only American national security but the democratic way of life itself was being threatened caused him to ponder often, publicly and privately, on the nature of democracy itself and on the restrictions it imposed on a President. To Frances Perkins he confided that a democratic leader needs, above all, patience. On one occasion he defined his "lesson in patience" that he had been giving her by saying, "You have to give men an opportunity to understand for themselves in their own way. You can't rush them. Not in a democracy."[30]

Therefore he used the method, as King George VI defined it, of "leading public opinion by allowing it to get ahead of [him]." Sometimes he tested public opinion through having members of his administration give "trial balloon" speeches, as for example the address of William Bullitt on August 18, 1940, just prior to the destroyers-for-bases deal. More often, he led public opinion by encouraging others to speak out in order to "goad" him into action. He was always careful not to take action or an advanced position simply because polls showed that he had a majority, or even a very large majority, in favor of such a stand. If the unity required for a total war effort were to be achieved, it was never enough just to have majority support. That majority, as his Lend-Lease administrator

Stettinius later explained, "had to be so strong and so determined that the will of the country was unmistakable to every citizen regardless of his own views."[31]

Possibly because there were so many complaints in his own day, Roosevelt has since been faulted by some historians for underestimating popular support for his foreign policy. They have also complained that he exaggerated the potency of the congressional opposition. The strength of the political opposition can be seen in the partisan voting pattern of Congress, observable in this period most especially in 1939 and the latter months of 1941. As far as public opinion is concerned, it was not a question of underestimating popular support. More to the point, he had a basic understanding of how to lead public opinion by allowing it to get ahead of him, in order for the country to achieve as nearly as possible a sense of purpose and unity of spirit.

Thus Roosevelt proceeded slowly and with infinite patience to prepare a country to be ready to fight for its survival. It must be conceded that he was not always candid, especially in the presentation of each new program in the 1939-1941 period as a step in the direction of peace rather than war. Undoubtedly he felt that this was the only way the programs could be assured public acceptance and congressional approval and the administration could avoid what would have been an extremely serious situation had any of its proposals met outright rejection. The natural American hatred of war was what Roosevelt both understood and with which he had to cope throughout this period. He could not have been as boldly outspoken in 1941 as Stimson wished him to be, or as Stimson thought T.R. would have been. The first Roosevelt had come on the scene at a time when the country was in a more bellicose mood and too far removed from the last major war to have had a recollection of the horrors of warfare. The second Roosevelt lived in an era that remembered World War I only too well and would not by choice go into the dark night of a second holocaust. He lived in a time beset with big problems and governed by gigantic events, but he was a leader equal to the challenges of his day. He dedicated himself to inspiring confidence, to educating the nation to the realization of the Nazi threat to its security, and to taking the steps necessary to enable this country to survive. Ultimately he proved to be a great wartime leader, but not the least important part of his contribution to the successful outcome of World War II was made in the difficult, critical prewar period of 1939-1941.

NOTES

[1] Roosevelt to Arthur Murray, April 14, 1933, Nixon (ed.), *Roosevelt and Foreign Affairs*, I, 54.
  In Roosevelt's discourse and writing, both public and private, the word "realist" creeps in time and time again. Associates and historians have described him more comprehensively, however, as a "practical idealist." See Range, *Roosevelt's World Order*, pp.30-35; also Sherwood, *Roosevelt and Hopkins*, p. 266. To Henry Steele Commager he was "a hard-headed realist who is yet a music maker and a dreamer of dreams." Commager, "America's Faith," p. 15.

[2] Schlesinger, Jr., "As the world moved toward war," p. 2; Hofstadter, *American Political Tradition*, p. 316.

[3] See Freidel, *Roosevelt: The Apprenticeship*, the volume that deals with the early stages of Roosevelt's career. In his subsequent volume, depicting Roosevelt in the decade of the twenties, Professor Freidel elucidated: "Yet while Roosevelt had dropped dramatically his Navy way of thinking about Japan, he persisted for several years in feeling much as he had earlier about Caribbean relations. This is understandable enough, since he had never been an isolationist, and being an internationalist did not seem incompatible with being an imperialist." Freidel. *Roosevelt: The Ordeal*, p. 135.

[4] Divine, *Roosevelt and World War II*, p. 51. Freidel, *Roosevelt: The Ordeal*, p. 17.

[5] Chadwin, *Hawks of World War II*, p. 23. Chadwin cites as sources Schlesinger, Jr., *The Age of Roosevelt: The Crisis of the Old Order*, Burns, *Roosevelt: The Lion and the Fox*, and Leuchtenburg, *Roosevelt and the New Deal*.

[6] Divine, *Reluctant Belligerent*, p. 3.

[7] Divine, *Roosevelt and World War II*, p. 56.

[8] Hofstadter, *American Political Tradition*, p. 317.

[9] Friedel, *Roosevelt: The Triumph*, p. 252.

[10] FDR to Robert Woolley, February 25, 1932, quoted in Freidel, *Roosevelt: The Triumph*, p. 253

[11] See especially Burns, *Roosevelt: The Lion and the Fox*, pp. 247-63; and also Hofstadter, *American Political Tradition*, pp. 338-39; Leuchtenburg, *Roosevelt and the New Deal*, pp. 197-211.

[12] Schlesinger, Jr., "As the world moved toward war," p.21.

[13] Welles, *Time for Decision*, p. 50; Langer and Gleason, *Challenge to Isolation*, pp.1-2.

[14] As stated to the writer by Raymond P. Brandt, Chief of the Washington Bureau of the *St. Louis Post-Dispatch*, 1934-1961, in an interview on August 12, 1969.

[15] Neustadt, *Presidential Power*, p. 162.

[16] Langer and Gleason, *Challenge to Isolation*, p. 3.

[17] Hugh Gibson to Roosevelt, September 4, 1934, Nixon (ed.), *Roosevelt and Foreign Affairs*, II, 205.

[18] William Phillips memoir, Columbia Oral History Collection, p. 130; Arthur Krock memoir, Columbia Oral History Collection, p. 30.

[19] Joseph C. Grew to Cordell Hull, May 11, 1933, FDRL, PSF Japan.

[20] Hornbeck memorandum, May 29, 1933, attached to the report of Joseph Grew to Cordell Hull, cited above, FDRL, PSF Japan.

[21] Hornbeck Précis on "Russo-Japanese Conflict," February 2, 1934, FDRL, PSF Japan.

[22] Leuchtenburg, *Roosevelt and the New Deal*, p. 206.

[23] Roosevelt to the Rev. Malcolm E. Peabody, August 19, 1933, FDRL, PPF 732.

[24] Roosevelt, "Shall We Trust Japan?" pp. 476, 478.

[25] Samuel I. Rosenman feels that Roosevelt's hostility toward Japan stemmed not so much from a pro-China attitude as from the fact that they were aggressors. As stated to the writer in an interview with Judge Rosenman, July 16, 1969.

[26] Farley, *Jim Farley's Story*, p. 39.

[27] Roosevelt confided to Dodd, "I do not know that the United states can save civilization but at least by our example we can make people think and give them the opportunity of saving themselves. The trouble is that the people of Germany, Italy and Japan are not given the privilege of thinking." FDR to William E. Dodd, December 2, 1935, Elliott Roosevelt (ed.), *Personal Letters*, I, 531.

[28] As stated to the writer in an interview with his daughter, Anna Roosevelt Halsted, October 29, 1969. Roosevelt, she emphasized, was most apprehensive of the threat posed by Hitler and Mussolini, because "he knew that they were mad."

[29] Memorandum from FDR to Stephen T. Early, dictated in answer to a question from D. S. Freeman of *The Richmond News Leader*, January 10, 1938, FDRL, PPF 5763.

[30] Roosevelt to John S. Lawrence, July 27, 1933, Roosevelt to Breckinridge Long, September 11, 1933, Nixon (ed.), *Roosevelt and Foreign Affairs*, I, 330, 394.

[31] Dodd surmised that the Germans themselves were concerned about the effect the persecutions were having on United States public opinion. "The people," Dodd wrote of the German leaders, "have never learned the give-and-take group compromises which English and American leaders always apply. They are much concerned here about United States attitudes, but hardly know how to ease down off their dangerous position. This applies especially to the Jewish persecutions." Dodd to Roosevelt, July 30, 1933, Nixon (ed.), *Roosevelt and Foreign Affairs*, I, 337.

For direct reports to Roosevelt and analyses of the persecutions see S. R. Fuller, Jr. to Roosevelt, May 11, 1933, and John F. Coar to Louis M. Howe, September 2, 1933, Nixon (ed.), *Roosevelt and Foreign Affairs*, I, 173-76, 384-85.

[32] Nixon (ed.), *Roosevelt and Foreign Affairs*, II, 492; Phillips, *Ventures in Diplomacy*, pp. 165-66.

[33] Arthur Krock memoir, Columbia Oral History Collection, pp. 41-46; Elliott Roosevelt (ed.), *Personal Letters*, I, 605-6; and the following items in Nixon (ed.), *Roosevelt and Foreign Affairs*, III: Mary E. Woolley to Roosevelt, August 10, 1936, p. 373, p. 373n; Dodd to Roosevelt, August 19, 1936, p. 391; Stephen Early to Marvin McIntyre, August 26, 1936, p. 401, p. 401n.

[34] Writer's interview with Anna Roosevelt Halsted, October 29, 1969.

[35] Freidel, *Roosevelt: The Apprenticeship*, pp. 33-34, 333, 371; *Roosevelt: The Ordeal*, p. 13.

[36] S. R. Fuller, Jr. to Roosevelt, May 11, 1933, George H. Earle to Roosevelt, November 27, 1933, Nixon (ed.), *Roosevelt and Foreign Affairs*, I, 174, 505.

[37] For Dodd's reports to Roosevelt, see Nixon (ed.), *Roosevelt and Foreign Affairs*, I-III, passim, and especially Dodd to Roosevelt, November 27, 1933, in Nixon (ed.), I, 507-9. For Consul General Messersmith's reports see the U.S. Department of State publication *Peace and War*. Undersecretary of State Phillips felt one letter from Messersmith significant enough to quote to Roosevelt. Messersmith had written:

I realize thoroughly that we want an outlet for raw materials and that Germany is potentially one of our best customers for such materials; but I am convinced that anything that we do now, directly or indirectly, will be of no real help to us and will merely aid to maintain a regime which is beginning to totter, and that the only hope for Europe, and for us all, is that this regime does fall so that it may be replaced by a Government with which we can deal in the ordinary way. . . . As I see it, we have nothing to lose and everything to gain by a policy of waiting———Quoted by Phillips to Roosevelt, June 5, 1934, Nixon (ed.), *Roosevelt and Foreign Affairs*, II, 140.

Roosevelt had a high opinion of both representatives in Berlin. He said of Messersmith, "He is one of the best men we have in the whole Service and I count greatly on his judgment." Roosevelt to Judge Julian W. Mack, December 4, 1935, Nixon (ed.), *Roosevelt and Foreign Affairs*, III, 111. He refused to let Dodd resign in 1935, asserting, "In any event, we most certainly do not want him to consider resigning. I need him in Berlin." Roosevelt to R. Walton Moore, September 11, 1935, Nixon (ed.), *Roosevelt and Foreign Affairs*, III, 6.

[38] Dodd to Roosevelt, October 13, 1933, Nixon (ed.), *Roosevelt and Foreign Affairs*, I, 425.

[39] Quoted in Schlesinger, Jr., "As the world moved toward war," p. 2.

[40] Gilbert, *Nuremberg Diary*, p. 177.

[41] Welles, *Time for Decision*, p. 29.

[42] An Appeal to the Nations of the World, May 16, 1933, Rosenman (ed.), *Public Papers*, II, 185; Frankfurter to Roosevelt, May 9, 1933, Nixon (ed.), *Roosevelt and Foreign Affairs*, I, 102.

[43] Nixon (ed.), *Roosevelt and Foreign Affairs*, I, 128; Hull, *Memoirs*, I, 226-27; Moley, *After Seven Years*, p. 214.

[44] On April 14, 1933 Roosevelt had stated to his distant cousin in England, Arthur Murray, "Things seem to be complicated a bit by the development in Germany but I still believe that in every country the people themselves are more peaceably and liberally inclined than their governments." Nixon (ed.), *Roosevelt and Foreign Affairs*, I, 54.

[45] Address before the Woodrow Wilson Foundation, December 28, 1933, Rosenman (ed.), *Public Papers*, II, pp. 544-49.

[46] Divine, *Reluctant Belligerent*, pp. 5-7; Hull, *Memoirs*, I, 227-30.

[47] Elliott Roosevelt (ed.), *Personal Letters*, I, 623; Divine, *Illusion of Neutrality*, p. 55.

[48] FDR to Edward M. House, April 10, 1935, Elliott Roosevelt (ed.), *Personal Letters*, I, 472-73.

[49] Freidel, *Roosevelt: The Ordeal*, p. 87.

[50] Divine, *Illusion of Neutrality*, p. 120.

[51] Divine, *Reluctant Belligerent*, pp. 17-18; for the Warren report, see R. Walton Moore to Roosevelt, August 27, 1934; for the President's memorandum to Hull, see Roosevelt to Cordell Hull, September 25, 1934, both in Nixon (ed.), *Roosevelt and Foreign Affairs*, II, 187-90 and 222.

[52] Pierrepont Moffat to William Phillips, April 19, 1935, Nixon (ed.), *Roosevelt and Foreign Affairs*, I, 56, 57n.

[53] Divine, *Reluctant Belligerent*, p. 18; Hull to Roosevelt, April 11, 1935, Nixon (ed.), *Roosevelt and Foreign Affairs*, II, 470-75; Divine, *Illusion of Neutrality*, pp. 87-88.

[54] Compare the Hull draft. Hull to Roosevelt, August 29, 1935, Nixon (ed.), *Roosevelt and Foreign Affairs*, II, 631, with the final version of the President's statement in *Peace and War*, pp. 271-72.

[55] Divine, *Reluctant Belligerent*, p. 22; Statement by President Roosevelt, August 31, 1935, *Peace and War*, p. 272.

[56] FDR to William E. Dodd, December 2, 1935, Elliott Roosevelt (ed.), *Personal Letters*, I, 530-31.

[57] Divine, *Reluctant Belligerent*, pp. 28, 37; Leuchtenburg, *Roosevelt and the New Deal*, p. 225.

[58] Cohen, *American Revisionists*, p. 160.

[59] Freidel, *Roosevelt: The Apprenticeship*, p. 250.

[60] Roosevelt to Oswald Garrison Villard, August 24, 1936, Nixon (ed.), *Roosevelt and Foreign Affairs*, III, 395.

[61] Nixon (ed.), *Roosevelt and Foreign Affairs*, III, 336-37; for an account of how the

Democratic platform was drafted see Rosenman, *Working with Roosevelt*, pp. 101-3.
[62] Freidel, *Roosevelt: The Apprenticeship*, p. 361; Rosenman, *Working with Roosevelt*, p. 108; Address at Chautauqua, N.Y., August 14, 1936, Rosenman (ed.), *Public Papers*, V, 289.
[63] William Phillips memoir, Columbia Oral History Collection, pp. 67, 100; Perkins, *The Roosevelt I Knew*, p. 29.
[64] Stated to the writer by Samuel I. Rosenman in an interview on July 9, 1969.
[65] Divine, *Reluctant Belligerent*, p. 31.
[66] Borg, "Notes on 'Quarantine' Speech," p. 413.
[67] There are various interpretations of what Roosevelt meant in the Quarantine speech. See Wiltz, *From Isolation to War*, pp. 62-63. Recently, Dorothy Borg has asserted that Roosevelt did not have a specific or dramatically new policy in mind, but was still "groping," as he had been for some time, for some kind of feasible peace plan. Borg, "Notes on 'Quarantine' Speech," pp. 405-24.

Miss Borg also makes quite evident that Roosevelt was concerned about more than just the Asian situation. In fact, it would seem, on the basis of evidence presented, that he was thinking primarily of Europe. Although a letter of Sumner Welles' in the fifties has been used to indicate that the word "quarantine" was inspired by Roosevelt's concern over Japanese aggression, Miss Borg cites an earlier statement by Welles, in 1944, when, as she says, he was "closer to the event", which indicates Roosevelt's main worry was still Hitler. In *The Time for Decision*, published in 1944, Welles wrote:

Partly because of the issues involved in the Spanish war, and partly because the real nature of Hitlerism was becoming increasingly apparent, the President determined to make a vigorous effort to persuade public opinion that in its own interest the United States should propose some constructive plan for international action to check the forces of aggression before they succeeded in engulfing the world. For this effort he selected the very heart of isolationism—the city of Chicago.——Quoted in Borg, "Notes on 'Quarantine' Speech," p. 418.

Benjamin V. Cohen, in an interview with the writer on October 28, 1969, stated also that Roosevelt was chiefly worried about Europe at the time of the Quarantine speech.
[68] There is some question about whether Roosevelt thought the general reaction bad or was merely upset by a virulent outburst from an isolationist minority. Although he and administration figures have made statements to the effect that there was overwhelming popular disapproval (see Borg, "Notes on 'Quarantine' Speech," p. 425; and Rosenman, *Working With Roosevelt*, pp. 166-67), yet Roosevelt also wrote to Colonel House, "I thought, frankly, that there would be more criticism. . . ." F.D.R. to Edward M. House, October 19, 1937, Elliott Roosevelt (ed.), *Personal Letters*, I, 719. Miss Borg suggests that the administration may have ignored, perhaps unconsciously, a large favorable response while being extremely sensitive to violent attacks from prominent isolationists, with the result that although "considerable evidence of approval of the speech came to the attention of the Administration, [it] was not accepted as weighing substantially in the balance." Borg, "Notes on 'Quarantine' Speech," pp. 424-33. William Y. Elliott suggests why this kind of thing could have happened:

On the other side, however, we must take into account the necessity which Presidents have felt to carry along an almost overwhelming support of public opinion before they would act. This has meant an inability or unwillingness to act against a 25 or 30 percent opposition of such strenuous character as to endanger success at the polls. . . . Note, for example, how Franklin D. Roosevelt soft-pedaled the 'Quarantine' idea after his challenging speech in 1937——Elliott and Assocs., *United States Foreign Policy*, p. 208.

[69] Rosenman, *Working With Roosevelt*, p. 167.
[70] Langer and Gleason, *Challenge to Isolation*, pp. 35-37.
[71] Rosenman (ed.), *Public Papers*, VII, 597.

CHAPTER 2

[1] Bullitt to Roosevelt, November 8, 1936, FDRL, PSF France.
[2] Adler, *Uncertain Giant*, pp. 202-5; Leuchtenburg, *Roosevelt and the New Deal*, p. 215; Divine, *Reluctant Belligerent*, pp. 42-43; Rosenman (ed.), *Public Papers*, VII, 68-71.
[3] Bullitt to Roosevelt, May 30, 1938, FDRL, PSF France; Roosevelt to Bullitt, November 28, 1939, FDRL, PSF Bullitt; Langer and Gleason, *Challenge to Isolation*, p. 46.
[4] Blum, *Years of Urgency*, p. 66.
[5] U.S. Department of War, *Chief of Staff: Prewar Plans and Preparations*, pp. 131-32.
[6] Bullitt to Roosevelt, September 10, 1938, FDRL, PSF Bullitt.
[7] Memo of Talk with F.D.R., January 14, 1939, Josephus Daniels Papers, Box 17, Library of Congress.
[8] U.S. Department of War, *Chief of Staff: Prewar Plans and Preparations*, pp. 126-27, 132-33, 136-38; Langer and Gleason, *Challenge to Isolation*, p. 38.
[9] Roosevelt to Stimson, February 6, 1935, Nixon (ed.), *Roosevelt and Foreign Affairs*, II, 397.
[10] Langer and Gleason, *Undeclared War*, p. 735; Sherwood, *Roosevelt and Hopkins*, p. 272.
[11] Langer and Gleason, *Challenge to Isolation*, p. 48.
[12] *Ibid*, pp. 48-50; Press Conference #523, February 3, 1939, Rosenman (ed.), *Public Papers*, VIII, 111-13; Jacob, "Influence of World Events on U.S. 'Neutrality' Opinion," p. 54.
[13] Conference 645-A. Conference with Members of the Business Advisory Council, Executive Office of the White House, May 23, 1940, FDRL, President's Press Conferences.
    Secretary of the Interior Harold Ickes noted in his Diary on January 29, 1939:

Yesterday I lunched with President again in the Oval Room in the White House. And once again we talked about the European situation. . . . He developed the theory that our first line of defense is really the small countries of Europe that have not yet been overwhelmed by the Nazis. He seriously thinks that if Hitler extends his power over these small countries and then uses the economic weapon that will be his, he will be striking a serious blow at us without even a thought of trying to land a soldier on these shores. There is no doubt that the President is seriously concerned about the situation.——Ickes, *Diary*, II, 571

[14] Rosenman (ed.), *Public Papers*, VIII, 3-4.
[15] Divine, *Reluctant Belligerent*, p. 57; Press Conference #518, Executive Offices of the White House, January 17, 1939, FDRL, President's Press Conferences.
[16] See R. Walton Moore to Roosevelt, March 18, 1939, FDRL, PSF Neutrality.
[17] For an excellent analysis of changing public opinion in the post-Munich period see Jacob, "Infuence of World Events on U.S. 'Neutrality' Opinion," pp. 48-65. Mr. Jacob comes to the conclusion that "the aftermath of Munich, not the dramatic march into Prague [March 1939], overturned American neutrality opinion, illustrating the importance of the cumulative effect of world events on opinion in contrast to the influence of particular events."
    See also Divine, *Reluctant Belligerent*, pp. 55, 59.
[18] Divine, *Illusion of Neutrality*, pp. 235-36; Hull, *Memoirs*, I, 613; Leuchtenburg, *Roosevelt and the New Deal*, pp. 252-54, 271-72.
[19] See Adler, *Isolationist Impulse*, pp. 295ff. for an excellent description of the changing elements in the isolationist coalition from 1939 through 1941. His most significant point is that liberals came out of the coalition after the spring blitzkrieg in 1940, leaving "the bitter right in almost complete control. The progressive strain, so significant in the older generation of American isolationists, all but disappeared."
[20] Cornelius Vanderbilt, Jr. to Missy LeHand, February 27 [1939], FDRL, PPF 104.
[21] Writer's interview with Adolf A. Berle, February 5, 1970; Jacob, "Influence of World Events on U.S. 'Neutrality' Opinion," pp. 58-61; Cantril (ed.), *Public Opinion*, pp. 975-77.
[22] Clyde Eagleton to Dr. Stanley K. Hornbeck, February 16, 1939, FDRL, PPF 1820.
[23] Charles Calmer Hart to Colonel Marvin H. McIntyre, February 6, 1939, FDRL, OF 3575.
[24] Sidney Sherwood to Roosevelt, March 24, 1939, FDRL, OF 3575.
[25] Rosenman, *Working With Roosevelt*, p. 182.

[26] In his preface, written in mid-1941, to the 1940 volume of *Public Papers* Roosevelt later said:

It has now become apparent that the very physical security of the United States is at stake. The United States has, in its history, been actively engaged in several wars with foreign nations; but now for the first time, even though not actually at war, its physical safety and independence are being threatened. It has also become clear that democracy itself, as an institution and as a way of life, is in the same danger. For the plan of the Nazis now appears in its true light—to dominate the entire world not only physically but ideologically. What the Nazis hope to accomplish—and they are trying to make good that hope—is the political and physical control of the entire world, and with it the imposition of their own so-called "new order."————Rosenman (ed.), *Public Papers* IX, xxviii.

As early as March 31, 1939 he had spoken in a press conference of "a general fear of an effort by the Nazis, to attain world dominance. . . . That is what is giving the world concern today." Roosevelt made this point as part of "a background story without attribution. . . . In other words, do not bring me into it." Press Conference #534, Warm Springs, Georgia, March 31, 1939, Rosenman (ed.), *Public Papers*, VIII, 185-86.

[27] Memo of Talk with F.D.R., January 14, 1939, Josephus Daniels Papers, Box 17, Library of Congress.

[28] Press Conference #540-A, American Society of Newspaper Editors, In the State Dining Room of the White House, April 20, 1939, FDRL, President's Press Conferences.

[29] Ickes, *Diary*, II, 568.

[30] For a discussion of this point and a presentation of the various viewpoints, see Frye, *Nazi Germany and the American Hemisphere*, pp. 3-14. Frye's conclusion is that an invasion of this hemisphere was a definite possibility. "It is difficult," he writes, "to escape the conclusion that, had the Nazis achieved enduring victory in the Old World, the nations of the New would have faced an unending succession of political assaults. And hindsight confirms what important elements in the Reich hierarchy had already come to expect—that technological progress would certainly make feasible a transatlantic attack in the near future." *Ibid*., p. vii.

[31] Press Conference #530-A, Executive Offices of the White House, March 17, 1939, FDRL, President's Press Conferences; Alsop and Kintner, *American White Paper*, p. 40.

[32] Langer and Gleason, *Challenge to Isolation*, p. 50; Divine, *Reluctant Belligerent*, pp. 58-62.

[33] Press Conference #555, Executive Offices of the White House, June 20, 1939, FDRL, President's Press Conferences.

[34] Connally and Steinberg, *My Name is Tom Connally*, p. 226.

[35] Press Conference #540-A, American Society of Newspaper Editors, In the State Dining Room of the White House, April 20, 1939, FDRL, President's Press Conferences.

[36] Hull, *Memoirs*, I, 647-48.

[37] Press Conference #560, Hyde Park, July 4, 1939, FDRL, President's Press Conferences.

[38] Press Conference #561, Executive Offices of the White House, July 11, 1939, FDRL, President's Press Conferences.

Langer and Gleason, in commenting on the eventual failure to repeal the arms embargo before the outbreak of the Second World War, feel that repeal would not have deterred Hitler. They do say, however, that "at the time the President, as well as many other statesmen, believed sincerely that a potent weapon for peace had been thrust aside." Langer and Gleason, *Challenge to Isolation*, pp. 146-47. Although this statement is correct as far as Cordell Hull is concerned (since their work is based primarily on the voluminous State Department records and papers of State Department officials, they were extremely cognizant of the point of view at that source), it is difficult to see how such a conclusion can be drawn for Roosevelt.

[39] Alsop and Kintner, *American White Paper*, pp, 40, 45; Hull, *Memoirs*, I, 649-50, 653.

[40] Joseph Alsop, a distant cousin of the Roosevelts and a Grotonian, corresponded with Eleanor Roosevelt and Steve Early in 1939 and 1940, advising them of the forthcoming publication of *American White Paper*, and received White House approval for his project. See Joseph Alsop to Eleanor Roosevelt, September 29, 1939 and Stephen Early to Roosevelt, February 23, 1940, FDRL, PPF 300.

Alsop and Kintner were given special help in the preparation of their manuscript by Assistant Secretary of State Adolf A. Berle, Jr., who was their State Department liaison. See the pps. of the manuscript sent to Steve Early by Joseph Alsop, February 23, 1940, FDRL, PPF 300.

[41] Alsop and Kintner, *American White Paper*, p. 46.

[42] Press Conference #564, July 21, 1939, Rosenman (ed.), *Public Papers*, VIII, pp. 390-93.

[43] Press Conference #570, August 8, 1939, Rosenman (ed.), *Public Papers*, VIII, 428-29.

[44] Alsop and Kintner, *American White Paper*, p. 18.

[45] Secretary of State Hull and Undersecretary Welles approved the message because they felt it might offer a way out of the April "crisis" and buy time for England and France. Alsop and Kinter, *American White Paper*, pp. 35-36.

[46] Langer and Gleason, *Challenge to Isolation,* p. 88.

[47] *Ibid.*, pp. 125-26.

CHAPTER 3

[1] Compton, *The Swastika and the Eagle*, p. 74.

[2] Leuchtenburg, *Roosevelt and the New Deal*, p. 84; also stated to the writer in an interview with Samuel I. Rosenman, July 9, 1969.

[3] The quotations are from Roosevelt's bitterest campaign speech, the Madison Square Garden speech of October 31, 1936. He reacted in that address to the open hostility of business by declaring angrily: "Never before in all our history have these forces been so united against one candidate as they stand today. They are unanimous in their hate for me—and I welcome their hatred." Rosenman (ed.), *Public Papers*, V, 568.

[4] Rosenman (ed.), *Public Papers*, VII, 566.

[5] Rosenman (ed.), *Public Papers*, VIII, 4-5.

[6] His daughter Anna has observed that he was distressed by the fact that in American cities there were enclaves of immigrants in certain parts of the city while "the Americans" lived elsewhere, and that he had even pointed this out in a speech as an undesirable condition. Writer's interview with Anna Roosevelt Halsted, October 29, 1969.

[7] See, for instance, Press Conference, January 5, 1934, Nixon (ed.), *Roosevelt and Foreign Affairs*, I, 577; Roosevelt to Senator Frederic C. Walcott, November 8, 1933, *Ibid.*, I, 468-69; Roosevelt to Nicholas Murray Butler, September 26, 1934; *Ibid.*, II, 222.

[8] Roosevelt to Bingham, July 11, 1935, *Ibid.*, II, 553.

[9] Farley, *Jim Farley's Story*, p. 199. [1]

[10] *Ibid.*, pp. 189, 361.

[11] Wheeler-Bennett, *King George VI,* pp. 371-74.

[12] *Ibid.*, p. 382.

[13] Eleanor Roosevelt, *This I Remember*, pp. 183-84.

[14] Roosevelt to King George VI, November 2, 1938, FDRL, PSF Great Britain: King and Queen; Roosevelt to Arthur Murray, July 10, 1939, FDRL, PSF Great Britain: Arthur Murray.

[15] Wheeler-Bennett, *King George VI*, pp. 385, 391-92.

[16] *Ibid.*, p. 388.

[17] *Ibid.*

[18] *Ibid.*, p. 391.

[19] Sherwood, *Roosevelt and Hopkins*, p. 252.

[20] Fireside Chat on the War in Europe, September 3, 1939, Rosenman (ed.), *Public Papers*, VIII, 463.

[21] Divine, *Illusion of Neutrality*, pp. 290-91.

[22] Memorandum (anonymous), marked "File—personal and private, September 15, 1939," FDRL, PSF Neutrality.

The memorandum was obviously considered important enough to go into the President's Secretary's File (Grace Tully's file), which is considered the most important of the files in the Roosevelt Library. During his lifetime this was Roosevelt's working file, where Miss Tully kept items that he wished to have at hand for ready reference.

[23] Very much emphasized by Samuel I. Rosenman, in an interview with the writer on July 9, 1969; see also Rosenman, *Working With Roosevelt*, p. 190.

[24] Langer and Gleason, *Challenge to Isolation*, p. 221.

[25] See Stephen Early to F.D.R., September 14, 1939, Elliott Roosevelt (ed.), *Personal Letters*, II, 921.

[26] Alsop and Kintner, *American White Paper*, p. 75; Divine, *Reluctant Belligerent*, p. 67.

[27] Stephen Early to Myron C. Taylor, September 6, 1939, FDRL, OF 1561: Neutrality File; see also Divine, *Reluctant Belligerent*, p. 67.

[28] Divine, *Illusion of Neutrality*, p. 292; for a breakdown in voting on the Vorys amendment by section and party, see work cited, pp. 273-74.

[29] Rosenman (ed.), *Public Papers*, VIII, 521.

[30] Langer and Gleason, *Challenge to Isolation*, pp. 138, 222.

[31] Hull, *Memoirs*, I, 684.

[32] A memo in the White House files in regard to Senate management of the debate reads as follows:

The Vice President says:
"Tell Barkely, Sherman Minton and Jim Byrnes to do two things.
1. To keep their mouths shut and to shut off debate.
2. Keep the ball going at least six hours a day for a week. If, at the end of a week, filibuster starts, have night sessions and move the convening hour from noon to 11:00 and run it through to 10:00 or 11:00 every night. . . ."--Memo to the President, September 21, 1939, FDRL, PSF Neutrality.

[33] Divine, *Reluctant Belligerent*, p. 68; Langer and Gleason, *Challenge to Isolation*, p. 220.

[34] Divine, *Illusion of Neutrality*, pp. 298-300.

[35] F.D.R. to R. Walton Moore, September 11, 1939, Elliott Roosevelt (ed.), *Personal Letters,*, II, 919.

[36] FDRL, OF 1561: Neutrality File.

[37] Johnson, *Battle Against Isolation*, p. 34.

[38] Johnson, *William Allen White's America*, pp. 5, 9.

[39] Divine, *Illusion of Neutrality*, pp. 303-6, *Reluctant Belligerent*, pp. 68-69.

[40] Divine, *Illusion of Neutrality*, pp. 301-2, 306-7, 325-27.

[41] Harold Ickes to Roosevelt, October 16, 1939, FDRL, PSF Neutrality.

[42] For tallies by section and by party, see Divine, *Illusion of Neutrality*, pp. 325, 330.

[43] F.D.R. to Lord Tweedsmuir, October 5, 1939, F.D.R. to Harold L. Ickes, Memorandum, September 16, 1939, Elliott Roosevelt (ed.), *Personal Letters*, II, 934, 922.

[44] Divine, *Reluctant Belligerent*, p. 67.

[45] Gleeck, "96 Congressmen Make Up Their Minds," pp. 3-24.

[46] Stated by Samuel I. Rosenman in an interview with the writer, July 9, 1969.

[47] Jacob, "Influence of World Events on U.S. 'Neutrality' Opinion," pp. 54-57.

[48] Hooker (ed.), *Moffat Papers*, p. 266; Cantril (ed.), *Public Opinion*, pp. 1158-59.

CHAPTER 4

[1] See synopsis of Gallup and Fortune polls for September and October, in Langer and Gleason, *Challenge to Isolation*, p. 218*n*

[2] F.D.R. to William Allen White, December 14, 1939, Elliott Roosevelt (ed.), *Personal Letters*, II, 967-68.

[3] Conrad W. Crooker to Stephen Early, November 4, 1939, and Stephen Early to Crooker, November 20, 1939, FDRL, OF 1561: Neutrality File.

[4] Welles, *Time for Decision*, pp. 73-74.

[5] Raymond Clapper Papers, Box 243, Library of Congress.

[6] Welles, *Time for Decision*, p. 73.

[7] Alsop and Kintner, *American White Paper*, Appendix I, p. 85.

[8] Welles, *Time for Decision*, p. 92.

[9] Writer's interview with Mr. Benjamin Welles, son of Sumner Welles, May 28, 1970.

[10] The leading exponent of this view has been Herbert Feis, former Economic Advisor to the State Department. See Langer and Gleason, *Challenge to Isolation*, p. 365n.

Confirmation of the threefold purpose of the mission has also been given by former Assistant Secretary of State Adolf A. Berle, Jr., who indicated, in an interview with the writer on February 5, 1970, that the mission was undertaken to gather information, to seek out possibilities for peace, and to see, at the same time, if there were any strength among the neutrals.

[11] As stated to the writer by Raymond P. Brandt, describing Welles' report of his trip to Washington columnists and newspaper bureau chiefs at a dinner meeting at the home of Eugene Meyer. Writer's interview with Mr. Brandt, August 12, 1970. In his Report to Cordell Hull, Welles wrote of von Ribbentrop, "I have rarely seen a man I disliked more." Cordell Hull Papers, Box 90, Library of Congress.

[12] It is Samuel Rosenman's impression that at this point Roosevelt conceded to himself the eventuality of U.S. intervention. As expressed to the writer in an interview with Judge Rosenman on July 9, 1969.

[13] Frightened reactions are referred to in Rosenman, *Working With Roosevelt*, p. 194. General press response to the May 16 speech, however, was that Roosevelt should have asked more from Congress for defense. See Davis and Lindley, *How War Came*, p. 51.

After the May 26 address Ickes recorded in his Diary the following conversation with Justice William O. Douglas:

What had particularly worried Bill was that Congressmen on the Hill have begun to express the conviction that the President, with respect to the international situation, might prove to be a Chamberlain. He feels as I do about the President's speech last Sunday night. As a matter of fact, everyone with whom I have talked has said that that speech was disappointing, except Ross McIntire, who, while not enthusiastic about it, thought it was adequate.——Ickes, *Diary*, III, 191.

[14] Rosenman (ed.), *Public Papers*, IX, 202-4.

[15] F.D.R. to Frank Knox, October 4, 1939, Elliott Roosevelt (ed.), *Personal Letters*, II, 933; Langer and Gleason, *Challenge to Isolation*, pp. 131, 170-72.

[16] Conference 645-A. Conference with Members of the Business Advisory Council, Executive Office of the White House, May 23, 1940, FDRL, President's Press Conferences; Langer and Gleason, *Challenge to Isolation*, pp. 477-78.

[17] Press Conference #647, May 28, 1940, Rosenman (ed.), *Public Papers*, IX, 247-48; Radway, "Administrative History of the Advisory Commission to the Council of National Defense," unpublished manuscript, p. 11.

[18] Note outlining chronological development of U.S. prewar mobilization, Rosenman (ed.), *Public Papers*, IX, p. 205.

[19] Address at the University of Virginia, June 10, 1940, Rosenman (ed.), *Public Papers*, IX, 264.

[20] Message to the Congress asking Additional Appropriations for National Defense, May 16, 1940, Rosenman (ed.), *Public Papers*, IX, 202.

[21] Julius Pratt has written: "It was in the declaration that 'we will extend to the opponents of force the material resources of this nation' that the President unequivocally abandoned any pretense of old-fashioned neutrality toward the wars in Europe and Asia. Increasingly from now on the position of the United States was that of a nonbelligerent." Pratt, *Cordell Hull* I, 346.

[22] Writer's interview with Anna Roosevelt Halsted, October 29, 1969; Address at the University of Virginia, June 10, 1940, Rosenman (ed.), *Public Papers*, IX, 261.

[23] Perkins, *The Roosevelt I Knew*, p. 352; Blum, *Years of Urgency*, p. 94; Davis and Lindley, *How War Came*, pp. 44, 49; Rosenman, *Working With Roosevelt*, pp. 194-95.

[24] Stated to the writer by Anna Roosevelt Halsted in an interview on October 29, 1969.

[25] Davis and Lindley, *How War Came*, pp. 95-96.

[26] As stated to the writer in an interview with Anna Roosevelt Halsted on October 29, 1969.

[27] Churchill, *Their Finest Hour*, pp. 24-25.

[28] Cole, *America First*, p. 7; White's remarks quoted in Johnson, *Battle Against Isolation*, p. 91. For the details of the formation of the Committee to Defend America by Aiding the Allies, see Johnson, *Battle Against Isolation*, pp. 62-71.

[29] Johnson, *Battle Against Isolation*, pp. 72-75.
[30] Rosenman (ed.), *Public Papers*, IX, 199-200.
[31] Draft, Three Fallacies, "Isolation," November 8, 1939, FDRL, PSF Neutrality.
[32] Johnson, *Battle Against Isolation*, p. 91.
[33] *Ibid.*, pp. 98-99.
[34] As stated to the writer by Benjamin V. Cohen, in an interview on October 28, 1969.
[35] F.D.R. to Frank Knox (recently appointed Secretary of the Navy), July 22, 1940, Elliott Roosevelt (ed.), *Personal Letters*, II, 1048-49; Langer and Gleason, *Challenge to Isolation*, pp. 745-46; writer's interview with Benjamin V. Cohen, who commented that Roosevelt felt it would be detrimental to national unity to have congressional debate over destroyers in this election year. Obviously, the President also felt that it would be politically inadvisable for himself and ultimately, if he lost the election, would imperil the future security of the country.
[36] Churchill, *Their Finest Hour*, pp. 401-2. Langer and Gleason point out that "the unparaphrased text in the State Department files varies somewhat. [The third sentence from the end reads;] 'This is a most important thing to do now, Mr. President.' " Langer and Gleason, *Challenge to Isolation*, p. 749n.
[37] Ickes, *Diary*, III, 291-93; Goodhart, *Fifty Ships*, pp. 153-56; Langer and Gleason, *Challenge to Isolation*, pp. 749-51.
[38] Interviews with Benjamin V. Cohen, October 28, 1969, and with former Senator Claude Pepper (now Congressman from Dade County, Florida), October 30, 1969.
[39] As stated to the writer by Benjamin V. Cohen, October 28, 1969.
[40] Langer and Gleason, *Challenge to Isolation*, pp. 756-57; Bullitt's speech quoted in Johnson, *Battle Against Isolation*, p. 104.
[41] Goodhart, *Fifty Ships*, pp. 177-79; Langer and Gleason, *Challenge to Isolation*, pp. 760-61.
[42] Press Conference #677, September 3, 1940, Rosenman (ed.), *Public Papers*, IX, 375-85.
[43] *Chicago Tribune*, September 4, 1940.
[44] Churchill, *Their Finest Hour*, p. 404.
[45] Eleanor Roosevelt, *This I Remember*, p. 221.
[46] Langer and Gleason, *Challenge to Isolation*, p. 765.
[47] Tully, *F.D.R. My Boss*, p. 244.

CHAPTER 5

[1] Copy of article for the *Sunday Express* by Raymond Gram Swing, for publication in London May 11, 1941, sent by Harry Hopkins to Grace Tully, May 15, 1941, FDRL, PPF 1820.
[2] Johnson, *Battle Against Isolation*, p. 82.
[3] Roosevelt to Lewis W. Douglas, June 7, 1940, FDRL, PPF 1914.
[4] Langer and Gleason, *Challenge to Isolation*, p. 776.
[5] King George VI to Roosevelt, June 3, 1941, FDRL, PSF Great Britain.
[6] Langer and Gleason, *Challenge to Isolation*, pp. 49, 511.
[7] Stimson and Bundy, *On Active Service*, p. 324.
[8] Murray L. Goldsborough to Roosevelt, April 15, 1939, FDRL, OF 3575.
[9] Early in the fight for neutrality repeal in the fall of 1939 Ickes had confided to his Diary:

The reactionary Democrats are coming through pretty fast and almost unanimously in support of the President's position. Jim Farley said that he thought even Senator Gerry, of Rhode Island, would be all right if left alone. Other Senators who have come across are Glass, Byrd, Bailey, Burke, and many others who normally have taken a position during the last few years against anything that the President wanted. The difficulty will be in holding some of the liberal Senators in line, but to offset this defection the Administration bill will receive support from some of the Republicans. . . .——Ickes, *Diary*, III, 27.

[10] Ickes, *Diary*, II, 717-18.
[11] Ickes, *Diary*, III, 23; Ickes "My Twelve Years With F.D.R.," p. 89. Landon, on his part, notes James MacGregor Burns in *Roosevelt: The Soldier of Freedom*, p. 38, was not at all

enthusiastic about coming into the cabinet, for he feared that in so doing he would be setting Roosevelt up for a third term.

[12] Knox to Roosevelt, December 15, 1939, Box I, Frank Knox Papers, Library of Congress.
[13] Eleanor Roosevelt herself raised this point. See Frank Knox to Mrs. Knox, June 5, 1940, Box 3, Frank Knox Papers, Library of Congress.
[14] As expressed to the writer by Anna Roosevelt Halsted in an interview on October 29, 1969.
[15] Roosevelt to Frank Knox, December 29, 1939, FDRL, PSF/Frank Knox.
[16] Although Knox had indicated in May that he was ready to accept the post of Secretary of the Navy, as late as four days before the President's call he wrote to his wife: "I have had no word of any kind from Washington and I am beginning to believe that I will not—and this produces a sense of personal relief rather than disappointment." Frank Knox to Annie Knox, June 15, 1940, Box 3, Frank Knox Papers, Library of Congress.

Stimson, while aware that he was being suggested for the post of Secretary of War, was even more astonished than Knox to receive the summons. "To say that Stimson was surprised," writes his biographer, "would be putting it mildly. . . . Like everyone else, he knew that the Secretary of War, Woodring, was at odds with both the President and large parts of the Army. . . . Some weeks before, he had heard from Grenville Clark that his name had been suggested for the job. Clark had coupled it with that of Judge Robert P. Patterson as Assistant Secretary. He knew too that this suggestion had reached the President. But that the President should have listened to it, and acted on it, was astonishing. His first reaction was to point out that he was approaching his seventy-third birthday. The President said he already know that, and added that Stimson would be free to appoint his own Assistant Secretary." Stimson and Bundy, *On Active Service*, p. 323.

[17] Cantril, "America Faces the War: A Study in Public Opinion," p. 395.
[18] Cole, *America First*, pp. 37, 81.
[19] *Ibid.*, p. 94.
[20] "Chicago was long an isolationist citadel, largely by reason of its hives of hyphenates," writes the historian Thomas A. Bailey, "and this huge concentration of isolationism was able to exert disproportionate political power." Bailey, *The Man in the Street*, p. 109.
[21] Cole, *America First*, pp. 10, 30-31, 104-30; Johnson, *Battle Against Isolation*, p. 165.
[22] Cole, *America First*, pp. 15-16.
[23] *Ibid.*, pp. 35-37, 40.
[24] Goldman, *Tragedy of Lyndon Johnson*, p. 386.
[25] Pearl Buck to Eleanor Roosevelt, December 12, 1941, FDRL, PPF 1820.
[26] For an excellent study of the Century Group and its reorganization in April 1941 into the Fight for Freedom Committee, see Chadwin, *Hawks of World War II*. An early and still authoritative account of the activities of the White Committee and the Century Group in the summer of 1940 was published by Charles G. Ross, a contributing editor of the *St. Louis Post-Dispatch*, in that newspaper's issue of September 22, 1940.
[27] Johnson, *Battle Against Isolation*, pp. 193-201; Chadwin, *Hawks of World War II*, p. 175.
[28] Cantril, "America Faces the War: A Study in Public Opinion," p. 402.
[29] *Ibid.*, p. 403.
[30] "Gallup and Fortune Polls," *Public Opinion Quarterly*, V (Fall 1941), 481; Cantril, Rugg, and Williams, "America Faces the War: Shifts in Opinion," pp. 651-56.
[31] "Gallup and Fortune Polls," *Public Opinion Quarterly*, V (Fall 1941), 476.
[32] Langer and Gleason, *Challenge to Isolation*, p. 771.
[33] Sherwood, *Roosevelt and Hopkins*, p. 188. A section of the Republican party platform read: "The Republican party stands for Americanism, preparedness and peace. We accordingly fasten upon the New Deal full responsibility for our unpreparedness and for the consequent danger of involvement in war." *New York Times*, June 27, 1940.
[34] Divine, *Reluctant Belligerent*, p. 86.
[35] Rosenman, *Working with Roosevelt*, p. 239.
[36] Rosenman (ed.), *Public Papers*, IX, 415.
[37] *Ibid.*, p. 517.
[38] To Robert S. Allen, who had written him a letter of advice, Roosevelt replied, on October 22, 1940: "Your suggestion that I stress peace is excellent, and I shall continue to do it with even greater emphasis. . . ."Elliott Roosevelt (ed.), *Personal Letters*, I, 1073.

[39] Rosenman, *Working With Roosevelt*, p. 242; Sherwood, *Roosevelt and Hopkins*, pp. 190-91, 201. Sherwood says unequivocally that by the end of the campaign "this was a fight that he [Roosevelt] despised."

For detailed presentations of the full strategy of the 1940 campaign see the accounts of these two members of Roosevelt's speech-writing team: Rosenman, *Working With Roosevelt*, pp. 222-55, and Sherwood, *Roosevelt and Hopkins*, pp. 184-201.

[40] Roosevelt to Samuel I. Rosenman, November 13, 1940, FDRL, PPF 64: Samuel I. Rosenman.

[41] Langer and Gleason, *Undeclared War*, pp. 209-10; Rosenman, *Working With Roosevelt*, pp. 240-41; Sherwood, *Roosevelt and Hopkins*, pp. 189-90.

[42] One of the foremost analysts of election results, Samuel Lubell, found that Roosevelt lost sharply in German-American communities of the Midwest and made surprising gains in Yankee New England, an interventionist sector of the country. Lubell, *Future of American Politics*, pp. 140-42.

See also Parmet and Hecht, *Never Again*, pp. 276-77.

[43] Rosenman (ed.), *Public Papers*, IX, 466.

[44] For a scholarly and factual account of the development of the Lend-Lease concept and of the passage of the act, see Kimball, *The Most Unsordid Act*. Chapter IV deals with the thinking of Roosevelt and key administration personnel in the one and a half month period from the election to mid-December 1940.

[45] Kimball, *The Most Unsordid Act*, p. 124.

[46] Press Conference #702, December 17, 1940, Rosenman (ed.), *Public Papers*, IX, 607; Sherwood, *Roosevelt and Hopkins*, p. 225.

[47] Fireside Chat on National Security, White House, Washington, D.C., December 29, 1940, Rosenman (ed.), *Public Papers*, IX, 635, 640.

[48] Quoted in Langer and Gleason, *Undeclared War*, p. 249.

[49] *Ibid.*, p. 251.

[50] Kimball, *The Most Unsordid Act*, p. 165; Davis and Lindley, *How War Came*, p. 120.

[51] See Rosenman, *Working With Roosevelt*, p. 271. In an interview with the writer on July 9, 1969, Judge Rosenman maintained that Roosevelt's concern for unity led him to *insist* on full public debate on Lend-Lease.

The Lend-Lease Administrator, Edward R. Stettinius, Jr., observed in his book, *Lend-Lease: Weapon for Victory*, p. 72, that "a bare majority was not enough for the destroyers-for-bases deal, and even less so for Lend-Lease six months later." In this history, written from inside the administration, he went on to explain, in phraseology that strikingly approximated Roosevelt's own feelings:

The majority had to be so strong and so determined that the will of the country was unmistakable to every citizen regardless of his own views. To have acted suddenly without thorough discussion might have left a dangerous cleavage among the American people at a time when unity among us was more important than ever before. Days and weeks of full and open debate were needed before there was that solid basis of unity in the minds and hearts of the people necessary for the momentous step we were about to take.

This is not the method by which a dictator builds an army for aggression. But it is the method by which the people of a freedom-loving nation unite behind their leaders to defend themselves against dictators and eventually to create the overwhelming power necessary to crush them.

[52] Rosenman (ed.), *Public Papers*, X, 61, 63.

[53] Release of the Public Opinion News Service, April 18, 1941, Raymond Clapper Papers, Box 214, Library of Congress..

[54] Cole, *America First*, pp. 49-50; Kimball, *The Most Unsordid Act*, p. 192.

[55] On November 3, 1939, in a final vote on the conference report the Senate had supported revision of neutrality by 55 to 24 and the House by 243 to 172, but only six Republicans in the Senate and nineteen in the House had been included in the pro groups. Langer and Gleason, *Challenge to Isolation*, p. 231.

The February 8 House vote on Lend-Lease saw 236 Democrats and 24 Republicans in favor; 25 Democrats, 135 Republicans, 3 Progressives, 1 Farmer-Labor, and 1 American Labor party member opposed. Langer and Gleason, *Undeclared War*, p. 276.

On March 8 the Senate vote registered 49 Democrats, 10 Republicans, and 1

Independent in favor; 13 Democrats, 17 Republicans, and 1 Progressive opposed. U.S., *Congressional Record*, 77th Cong., 1st Sess., 1941, LXXXVII, Part 2, 2097.

The final House vote on March 11 saw 220 Democrats, 94 Republicans, and 3 Progressives in favor; 14 Democrats, 55 Republicans, 1 Farmer-Labor, and 1 American Labor party member opposed. U.S., *Congressional Record*, 77th Cong., 1st Sess., 1941, LXXXVII, Part 2, 2178.

[56] A good presentation of opposition arguments is given in Kimball, *The Most Unsordid Act*, pp. 154-55, 171-94.

[57] Davis and Lindley, *How War Came*, p. 115.

[58] Pratt, *Cordell Hull*, I, 356.

[59] For administration arguments, see Kimball, *The Most Unsordid Act*, pp. 165-88; Langer and Gleason, *Undeclared War*, pp. 262-68; Stettinius, *Lend-Lease*, pp. 77-79.

[60] Roosevelt to Marguerite M. Wells, March 4, 1941, FDRL, PPF 1439.

[61] Address at Annual Dinner of White House Correspondents' Association, March 15, 1941, Rosenman (ed.), *Public Papers*, X, 63-65.

[62] Clapper, *Watching the World*, pp. 268-70.

CHAPTER 6

[1] Twohey, "An Analysis of Newspaper Opinion on War Issues," p. 452.

[2] See comments on the vocal critics in Bernard De Voto to Elmer Davis, July 21, 1940, Elmer Davis Papers, Box I, Library of Congress.

[3] To the question, "Do you think the United States will go into the war in Europe sometime before it is over, or do you think we will stay out?" the "go in" answers from May 1940 to May 1941 ranged from 59 percent to 85 percent. In the first five months of 1941 the range was from 72 percent to 85 percent. "Gallup and Fortune Polls," *Public Opinion Quarterly*, V (Fall 1941) 476.

[4] Writer's interview, August 14, 1969, with Thomas G. Corcoran, who was very active in the administration in the years 1936 to 1940. He indicated that this was the way policy was made at the highest levels in the Roosevelt administration in those years immediately preceding Pearl Harbor.

[5] In early January Robert Kintner reported to Missy LeHand: "I cannot resist the temptation to write you about the two recent addresses of the President, the fireside chat and the talk on the state of the union. I, of course, thought both of them magnificent, but what I think is very unimportant. However, you might be interested in the fact that I have talked with a great many people—in Congress, in the Executive Branch and the businessmen now in Washington, and except for very rabid isolationists have found a remarkable unanimity in approval of the President's leadership." Kintner to Missy LeHand, January 7, 1941, FDRL, PPF 300: Joseph W. Alsop.

Kintner's observations are corroborated by the evidence in files in the Roosevelt Library, which contain many items of correspondence voicing enthusiastic approval of the two speeches.

[6] Lamont, who had just rendered valuable service in mobilizing forces for the passage of the Lend-Lease Act, was in frequent contact with the White House, sending words of advice on attitudes and procedures. The quotation cited above is from 1 Cor. 14:8 and is contained in Lamont's letter to Roosevelt, May 19, 1941, FDRL, PPF 1820.

[7] Telegram, Pierre Jay to the President, April 20, 1941, FDRL, PPF 619.

[8] Cornelius Vanderbilt Jr. to Missy LeHand, April 26 [1941], FDRL, PPF 104.

[9] See Diary entry for June 15, 1940, in Ickes, *Diary*, III, 209; Landecker, *The President and Public Opinion*, pp. 39-40.

[10] Langer and Gleason cite an "indiscreet" remark by Secretary Knox made privately in October 1940 to American officials planning aid to England. "I should like to say . . . I can't escape saying that the English are not going to win this war without our help, I mean our military help. . . . We needn't talk of it outdoors, but I think it true."——— Langer and Gleason, *Undeclared War*, p. 187.

Stimson's first clear expression of this belief was a confidence made to his Diary on December 16, 1940. His biographer, McGeorge Bundy, notes that "it was after the election, as the year was ending, that Stimson first noted in his diary his feeling that in the end the United States must fight. On December 16, after a meeting with Knox, General Marshall, and Admiral Stark, he noted that 'there was a basic agreement among us all. That in itself was very encouraging. All four agreed that this emergency could hardly be passed over without this country being drawn into the war eventually.' "————Stimson and Bundy, *On Active Service*, pp. 365-66.

[11] Blum, *Years of Urgency*, p. 253.

[12] On the night of Roosevelt's Arsenal of Democracy speech of December 29, 1940 Stimson wrote in his Diary that Americans could not indefinitely be "toolmakers for other nations which fight." He added, however, "That cannot yet be broached but it will come in time I feel certain and the President went as far as he could at the present time."————Stimson and Bundy, *On Active Service*, p. 366.

[13] *Ibid.*, pp. 366-76.

[14] Henry L. Stimson to Roosevelt, May 24, 1941, FDRL, PPF 1820. It appears that the underlining was done by Stimson.

[15] As recalled by Benjamin V. Cohen in an interview with the writer, October 28, 1969.

[16] Hofstadter, *American Political Tradition*, p. 265n.

[17] Sherwood, *Roosevelt and Hopkins*, pp. 292-93; Langer and Gleason, *Undeclared War*, pp. 458-59.

[18] Langer and Gleason, *Undeclared War*, p. 423.

[19] *Ibid.*, p. 443.

[20] Divine, *Reluctant Belligerent*, pp. 109-11; Langer and Gleason, *Undeclared War*, pp. 444-50.

[21] Churchill, *The Grand Alliance*, p. 140.

[22] A Radio Address Announcing the Proclamation of an Unlimited National Emergency, May 27, 1941, Rosenman (ed.), *Public Papers*, X, 188-94.

[23] Sherwood, *Roosevelt and Hopkins*, pp. 296-97.

[24] Langer and Gleason, *Undeclared War*, pp. 461-62.

[25] Sherwood, *Roosevelt and Hopkins*, p. 298.

[26] This cogent analysis is that of Anna Roosevelt Halsted, who expressed the Roosevelt political acumen very well in an interview with the writer on October 29, 1969.

[27] As expressed by Benjamin V. Cohen in an interview with the writer, October 28, 1969.

[28] Judge Rosenman feels that the activities of the German battleship *Bismarck* and the possibility that she might appear in the Caribbean, compelling Roosevelt to order the American navy into action against her, prompted Roosevelt to want to include a declaration of unlimited national emergency in this speech. According to Rosenman, "A declaration of an unlimited national emergency would at least create a better atmosphere for drastic action if he should decide to take it." Rosenman, *Working With Roosevelt*, p. 283.

Although the *Bismarck* was sunk on the day of the speech, the declaration might still be desirable in order to cover like developments in the near future.

Also, for a long time there had been talk both inside and out of administration circles that a declaration of an unlimited emergency was necessary in order to speed up a lagging war production.

[29] Cole, *America First*, p. 157.

[30] Twohey, "An Analysis of Newspaper Opinion on War Issues," p. 454.

[31] F.D.R. to Colonel and Mrs. Arthur Murray, June 2, 1941, Elliott Roosevelt (ed.), *Personal Letters*, II, 1165.

[32] Sherwood, *Roosevelt and Hopkins*, p. 293.

[33] Cantril (ed.), *Public Opinion*, p. 974; "Gallup and Fortune Polls," *Public Opinion Quarterly*, V (Fall 1941), 481.

[34] Twohey, "An Analysis of Newspaper Opinion on War Issues," pp. 448-55.

[35] "Gallup and Fortune Polls," *Public Opinion Quarterly*, V (Fall 1941), 485.

[36] To the question, "Should the United States government supply Russia with arms, airplanes, and other war materials on the same basis that we supply them to Britain?" only 35 percent answered "yes." Cantril (ed.), *Public Opinion*, p. 411.

[37] Divine, *Reluctant Belligerent*, pp. 125-29; Dawson, *Decision to Aid Russia*, pp. 138-43.

[38] Divine, *Reluctant Belligerent*, p. 127; Cantril (ed.), *Public Opinion*, p. 1128.

[39] Twohey, "An Analysis of Newspaper Opinion on War Issues," pp. 449, 453-55.

[40] As told by James P. Warburg, a former member of Roosevelt's early New Deal administration and then a Fight For Freedom member, in his book, *The Long Road Home*, p. 187.

[41] Sherwood, *Roosevelt and Hopkins*, p. 303.

[42] Telegrams, Robert Sherwood to Stephen T. Early, June 16, 1941, Stephen Early to Robert Sherwood, June 18, 1941, FDRL, OF 4461: Fight for Freedom Committee.

[43] Telegram to the President from Ulric Bell, November 24, 1941, Memorandum for Hon. Lowell Mellett from M. H. McIntyre, October 25, 1941, FDRL, OF 4461: Fight for Freedom Committee.

[44] Sherwood, *Roosevelt and Hopkins*, pp. 382-83; Cole, *America First*, pp. 64-68.

[45] Memorandum for Mr. Hassett from Paul Porter, November 12, 1941 (pencilled date, by member of White House staff), FDRL, OF 3575.

[46] Memorandum for the Vice President from FDR, November 6, 1941, H.A. Wallace to the President, November 8, 1941, Roosevelt to Wallace, November 11, 1941, FDRL, OF 3575.

[47] "The central responsibility of the Office of Facts and Figures," explains Samuel Rosenman about the agency that was established by executive order on October 24, 1941, "was to furnish the President with the background domestic intelligence he needed to make decisions on public information matters, and to present to the American people the most accurate and coherent accounts of governmental policy and international developments. To accomplish these purposes, the O.F.F. was designed to be a small advisory agency rather than a central information agency of the operational type." Rosenman (ed.), *Public Papers*, X, 428.
Roosevelt was opposed to the establishment of a major agency for dissemination of propaganda domestically, prior to American entry into World War II. See Ickes, *Diary*, III, 588-89; Chadwin, *Hawks of World War II*, p. 203n.

[48] Archibald MacLeish to Grace Tully, December 2, 1941, FDRL, OF 3575.

[49] Divine, *Reluctant Belligerent*, pp. 129-31.

[50] The latter interpretation was astutely expressed by a member of Congress to Benjamin V. Cohen and related to the writer by Mr. Cohen in an interview on October 28, 1969.

[51] Time and again interviewees have brought this point home to the writer.

[52] Fireside Chat to the Nation, September 11, 1941, Rosenman (ed.), *Public Papers*, X, 384-92.

[53] Navy and Total Defense Day Address, October 27, 1941, Rosenman (ed.), *Public Papers*, X, 438-44.

[54] Divine, *Reluctant Belligerent*, pp. 145-47.

CHAPTER 7

[1] Stimson and Bundy, *On Active Service*, p. 374.

[2] Langer and Gleason, *Undeclared War*, p. 521. Ickes also observed in his Diary entry of May 25, 1941: "The President said: 'I am not willing to fire the first shot.' So it seems that he is still waiting for the Germans to create an 'incident.' He indicated this on the fishing trip and since on two or three occasions."——Ickes, *Diary*, III, 523.
Langer and Gleason report that after the Cabinet meeting of May 23, 1941 "several members of the Cabinet came away with a feeling that Mr. Roosevelt was hoping for an incident in the Atlantic which would free him from his dilemma."——*Undeclared War*, p. 458. But the authors go on to comment that such expressions by Roosevelt were probably the result of "a fleeting mood of despair," that there were many incidents that summer, and had Roosevelt been serious about taking advantage of incidents to provoke a call for war he would have made much more of them than he did.

[3] Divine, *Reluctant Belligerent*, p. 145; Trefousse, *Germany and American Neutrality*, pp. 119-21.

[4] Langer and Gleason, *Undeclared War*, pp. 221-23, 285-89; Sherwood, *Roosevelt and*

Hopkins, pp. 271-74; U.S. Department of War, *Chief of Staff: Prewar Plans and Preparations*, pp. 119-25, 374ff; Burns, *Roosevelt: The Soldier of Freedom*, pp. 84-87.
[5]Davis and Lindley, *How War Came*, p. 10.
[6]Roosevelt terminology in Special Press Conference, December 20, 1940, Rosenman (ed.), *Public Papers*, IX, 625.
[7]As quoted by Roosevelt from Executive Order No. 8629 in his Press Conference #780, January 7, 1941, Rosenman (ed.), *Public Papers*, IX, 680-81.
[8]Rosenman (ed.), *Public Papers*, X, 353-54.
[9]*Ibid.*, pp. 354-59.
[10]Sherwood, *Roosevelt and Hopkins*, pp. 474-477.
[11]Harry Hopkins wrote in January 1942:

The truth of the matter is that production has gone pretty well, except in the conversion of plants and there the Government bumped head on into the selfish interests of big business, who refused to turn their hand unless they were forced to. The Army and Navy have been short-sighted and Congress has never seen the need of all-out production——Sherwood, *Roosevelt and Hopkins*, p. 476.

T. Harry Williams, Richard N. Current, and Frank Freidel, in their textbook *A History of the United States Since 1865* (New York: Alfred A. Knopf, 1969), p. 585, point out:

At the time of Pearl Harbor, the United States still possessed little armament because it had shipped so much to Great Britain and because so many plants had only recently begun production. [But, they add,] new productive capacity was remarkably large. Despite errors and chaotic conditions, the United States was producing more combat munitions than any of the belligerent nations—indeed almost as much as Germany and Japan combined.

[12]Langer and Gleason, *Undeclared War*, p. 440.
[13]Radway, "Administrative History of the Advisory Commission to the Council of National Defense." unpublished manuscript, p. 321.
[14]Press Conference #647, May 28, 1940, Rosenman (ed.), *Public Papers*, IX, 242.
[15]Perkins, *The Roosevelt I Knew*, p. 356.
[16]From his letter to William Allen White, *supra*, chap. iv, p. 54-55.
[17]Fireside Chat on National Defense, May 26, 1940, Rosenman (ed.), *Public Papers*, IX, 232, 235-36, 237-38.
[18]Sherwood, *Roosevelt and Hopkins*, pp. 187-88.
[19] Address at Annual Dinner of White House Correspondents' Association, March 15, 1941, Rosenman (ed.), *Public Papers*, X, 64-65.
[20]Tugwell, *The Democratic Roosevelt*, p. 349.
[21] Sherwood, *Roosevelt and Hopkins*, p. 282.
[22]Rossiter, *The American Presidency*, p. 150.
[23]Rosenman (ed.), *Public Papers*, IX, 212.
[24]Nelson, *Arsenal of Democracy*, p. 85.
[25] Frances Perkins writes: "One of the earliest acts indicating that the President foresaw the likelihood of war was his revival of the National Defense Council. By an Executive Order in May 1940 he declared that an emergency existed and revived this council provided for under law."——Perkins, *The Roosevelt I Knew*, p. 355.
[26]Bernard De Voto to Elmer Davis, July 21, 1940, Elmer Davis Papers, Box I, Library of Congress.
[27]Ickes, *Diary*, III, 511.
[28]Stimson and Bundy, *On Active Service*, p. 369.
[29]*Ibid.*, p. 374.
[30]Perkins, *The Roosevelt I Knew*, p. 343.
[31]Stettinius, *Lend-Lease*, p. 72.

BIBLIOGRAPHY

MANUSCRIPT COLLECTIONS

The most important source for the purpose of this study was the Franklin
D. Roosevelt Papers at the Franklin D. Roosevelt Library (FDRL), Hyde Park,
New York.
The major subdivision of the collections are

Official File (OF)
President's Personal File (PPF)
President's Secretary File (PSF)

Transcripts of the President's press conferences, on file at the Franklin D.
Roosevelt Library, were also consulted.

OTHER COLLECTIONS

The Manuscript Division, Library of Congress:

Raymond Clapper Papers
George F. Creel Papers
Josephus Daniels Papers
Elmer Davis Papers
Norman Davis Papers
William E. Dodd Papers
Cordell Hull Papers
Frank Knox Papers
Breckinridge Long Papers
Charles L. McNary Papers
Key Pittman Papers
William Allen White Papers

Oral History Collection, Columbia University: transcripts of interviews with
the following:

Arthur Krock
Emory S. Land

Herbert Claiborne Pell
William Phillips
Norman Thomas
James W. Wadsworth
James P. Warburg

BOOKS AND PAMPHLETS

Acheson, Dean. *Morning and Noon: A Memoir.* Boston: Houghton Mifflin Co., 1965.

————. *Present at the Creation: My Years in the State Department.* New York: W.W. Norton & Co., 1969.

Adler, Selig. *The Isolationist Impulse: Its Twentieth-Century Reaction.* London and New York: Abelard-Schuman, 1957.

————. *The Uncertain Giant, 1921-1941: American Foreign Policy Between the Wars.* New York: Macmillan Co., 1965.

Almond, Gabriel A. *The American People and Foreign Policy.* New York: Frederick A. Praeger, 1960.

Alsop, Joseph, and Robert Kintner. *American White Paper.* New York: Simon and Schuster, 1940.

Bailey, Thomas A. *The Man in the Street: The Impact of American Public Opinion on Foreign Policy.* New York: Macmillan Co., 1948.

Binkley, Wilfred E. *President and Congress.* New York: Alfred A. Knopf, 1947.

Bloom, Sol. *The Autobiography of Sol Bloom.* New York: G.P. Putnam's Sons, 1948.

Blum, John Morton. *From the Morgenthau Diaries.* Vol. II: *Years of Urgency, 1938-1941.* Boston: Houghton Mifflin Co., 1965.

Bullock, Alan. *Hitler: A Study in Tyranny.* Rev. ed. New York: Harper & Row, 1962.

Burns, James MacGregor. *Roosevelt: The Lion and the Fox.* New York: Harcourt, Brace & World, 1956.

————. *Roosevelt: The Soldier of Freedom.* New York: Harcourt Brace Jovanovich, 1970.

Butler, J.R.M. *Lord Lothian.* London: Macmillan & Co., 1960.

Cantril, Hadley. (ed.). *Public Opinion, 1935-1946.* Princeton: Princeton University Press, 1951.

Chadwin, Mark Lincoln. *The Hawks of World War II.* Chapel Hill: University of North Carolina Press, 1968.

Churchill, Winston S. *The Second World War: Their Finest Hour.* Boston: Houghton Mifflin Co., 1949.

————. *The Second World War: The Grand Alliance.* Boston: Houghton Mifflin Co., 1950.

Clapper, Raymond. *Watching the World.* New York: McGraw-Hill Book Co., 1944.

Cohen, Warren I. *The American Revisionists: The Lessons of Intervention in World War I.* Chicago and London: University of Chicago Press, 1967.

Cole, Wayne S. *America First: The Battle Against Intervention, 1940-1941.*

Madison: University of Wisconsin Press, 1953.

Compton, James V.   *The Swastika and the Eagle: Hitler, the United States, and the Origins of World War II.* Boston: Houghton Mifflin Co., 1967.

Connally, Tom, and Alfred Steinberg.   *My Name is Tom Connally.* New York: Thomas Y. Crowell Co., 1954.

Corwin, Edward S., and Louis W. Koenig.   *The Presidency Today.* New York: New York University Press, 1956.

Craig, Gordon A., and Felix Gilbert.   *The Diplomats, 1919-1939.* Princeton: Princeton University Press, 1953.

Current, Richard N.   *Secretary Stimson: A Study in Statecraft.* New Brunswick: Rutgers University Press, 1954.

Davis, Forrest, and Ernest K. Lindley.   *How War Came: An American White Paper, from the Fall of France to Pearl Harbor.* New York: Simon and Schuster, 1942.

Dawson, Raymond H.   *The Decision to Aid Russia, 1941: Foreign Policy and Domestic Politics.* Chapel Hill: University of North Carolina Press, 1959.

Divine, Robert A.   *The Illusion of Neutrality.* Chicago: University of Chicago Press, 1962.

————.   *The Reluctant Belligerent: American Entry into World War II.* New York: John Wiley & Sons, 1965.

————.   *Roosevelt and World War II.* Baltimore: Johns Hopkins Press, 1969.

Drummond, Donald F.   *The Passing of American Neutrality, 1937-1941.* Ann Arbor: University of Michigan Press, 1955.

Elliott, William Y., and Assocs.   *United States Foreign Policy: Its Organization and Control.* New York: Columbia University Press, 1952.

Farley, James A.   *Jim Farley's Story: The Roosevelt Years.* New York and Toronto: Whittlesey House, McGraw-Hill Book Co., 1948.

Feis, Herbert.   *The Road to Pearl Harbor: The Coming of the War Between the United States and Japan.* Princeton: Princeton University Press, 1950.

Freidel, Frank.   *Franklin D. Roosevelt: The Apprenticeship.* Boston: Little, Brown and Co., 1952.

————.   *Franklin D. Roosevelt; The Ordeal.* Boston: Little, Brown and Co., 1954.

————.   *Franklin D. Roosevelt: The Triumph.* Boston: Little, Brown and Co., 1956.

Friedländer, Saul.   *Prelude to Downfall: Hitler and the United States, 1939-1941.* Translated by Aline B. and Alexander Werth. New York: Alfred A. Knopf, 1967.

Frye, Alton.   *Nazi Germany and the American Hemisphere, 1933-1941.* New Haven and London: Yale University Press, 1967.

Gardner, Lloyd C. *Economic Aspects of New Deal Diplomacy.* Madison: University of Wisconsin Press, 1964

Gilbert, G. M.   *Nuremberg Diary.* New York: Farrar, Straus and Co., 1947.

Goldman, Eric F.   *The Tragedy of Lyndon Johnson.* New York: Alfred A. Knopf, 1969.

Goodhart, Philip.   *Fifty Ships that Saved the World.* New York: Doubleday and Co., 1965.

Graebner, Norman A. (ed.). *An Uncertain Tradition: American Secretaries of State in the Twentieth Century*. New York: McGraw-Hill, 1961

Grew, Joseph C. *Ten Years in Japan*. New York: Simon and Schuster, 1944.

Gunther, John. *Roosevelt in Retrospect: A Profile in History*. New York: Harper & Bros., 1950.

Hofstadter, Richard. *The American Political Tradition*. New York: Alfred A. Knopf, 1948.

Hooker, Nancy Harvison (ed.). *The Moffat Papers: Selections from the Diplomatic Journals of Jay Pierrepont Moffat*. Cambridge: Harvard University Press, 1956.

Hull, Cordell. *The Memoirs of Cordell Hull*. 2 vols. New York: Macmillan Co., 1948.

Ickes, Harold L. *The Secret Diary of Harold L. Ickes.* 3 vols. New York: Simon and Schuster, 1954.

Israel, Fred L. (ed). *The War Diary of Breckinridge Long: Selections from the Years 1939-1944*. Lincoln: University of Nebraska Press, 1966.

Johnson, Walter. *The American President and the Art of Communication*. Oxford: Clarendon Press, 1958.

————. *The Battle Against Isolation*. Chicago: University of Chicago Press, 1944.

————. *William Allen White's America*. New York: Henry Holt and Co., 1947.

Jonas, Manfred. *Isolationism in America, 1935-1941*. Ithaca: Cornell University Press, 1966.

Kimball, Warren F. *The Most Unsordid Act: Lend-Lease 1939-1941*. Baltimore: Johns Hopkins Press, 1969.

Landecker, Manfred. *The President and Public Opinion: Leadership in Foreign Affairs*. Washington D.C.: Public Affairs Press, 1968.

Langer, William L., and S. Everett Gleason. *The Challenge to Isolation, 1937-1940*. New York: Harper & Bros., 1952.

————. *The Undeclared War, 1940-1941*. New York: Harper & Bros., 1953.

Lash, Joseph P. *Eleanor Roosevelt: A Friend's Memoir*. Garden City, N.Y.: Doubleday & Co., 1964.

Leuchtenburg, William E. *Franklin D. Roosevelt and the New Deal*. New York: Harper & Row, 1963.

Lindley, Ernest K. *Half-Way With Roosevelt*. n.p.: Viking Press, 1936.

Loewenheim, Francis L. (ed.). *The Historian and the Diplomat: The Role of History and Historians in American Foreign Policy*, New York: Harper & Row, 1967.

Lubell, Samuel. *The Future of American Politics*. New York: Doubleday and Co., 1955.

Moley, Raymond. *After Seven Years*. New York and London: Harper & Bros., 1939.

Morison, Elting E. *Turmoil and Tradition: A Study of the Life and Times of Henry L. Stimson*. Boston: Houghton Mifflin Co., 1960.

Morison, Samuel Eliot. *History of United States Naval Operations in World War II*. Vol. I: *The Battle of the Atlantic, September 1939-May 1943*. Boston: Little, Brown and Co., 1961.

Nelson, Donald N.   *Arsenal of Democracy: The Story of American War Production.* New York: Harcourt, Brace, and Co., 1946.

Neustadt, Richard E.   *Presidential Power: The Politics of Leadership.* New York and London: John Wiley & Sons, 1960.

Nixon, Edgar B. (ed.).   *Franklin D. Roosevelt and Foreign Affairs.* 3 vols. Cambridge: Harvard University Press, 1969.

Parmet, Herbert S., and Hecht, Marie B.   *Never Again: A President Runs for a Third Term.* New York: Macmillan Co., 1968.

Perkins, Frances.   *The Roosevelt I Knew.* New York: Viking Press, 1946.

Phillips, William.   *Ventures in Diplomacy.* Boston: Beacon Press, 1952.

Pollard, James E.   *The Presidents and the Press.* New York: Macmillan Co., 1947.

Pratt, Julius W.   *Cordell Hull, 1933-1944.* Vols. XII and XIII of *The American Secretaries of State and Their Diplomacy,* ed. by Samuel Flagg Bemis. New York: Cooper Square Publishers, 1964.

Range, Willard.   *Franklin D. Roosevelt's World Order.* Athens: University of Georgia Press, 1959.

Roosevelt, Eleanor.   *This I Remember.* New York: Harper & Bros., 1949.

Roosevelt, Elliott.   *As He Saw It.* New York: Duell, Sloan and Pearce, 1946.

_____.(ed.).   *F.D.R.: His Personal Letters, 1928-1945.* 2 vols. New York: Duell, Sloan and Pearce, 1950.

Rosenman, Samuel I. (ed.).   *The Public Papers and Addresses of Franklin D. Roosevelt.* 13 vols. New York: I-V: Random House, 1938; VI-IX: Macmillan Co., 1941; X-XIII: Harper & Bros., 1950.

_____.   *Working With Roosevelt,* New York: Harper & Bros., 1952.

Rossiter, Clinton. *The American Presidency.* New York: Harcourt, Brace & World, 1960

Schlesinger, Arthur M., Jr.   *The Age of Roosevelt: The Coming of the New Deal.* Boston: Houghton Mifflin Co., 1958.

_____.   *The Age of Roosevelt: The Crisis of the Old Order, 1919-1933.* Boston: Houghton Mifflin Co., 1957.

Sherwood, Robert E.   *Roosevelt and Hopkins: An Intimate History.* New York: Harper & Bros., 1950.

Stettinius, Edward R., Jr.   *Lend-Lease: Weapon for Victory.* New York: Macmillan Co., 1944.

Stimson, Henry L., and McGeorge Bundy.   *On Active Service in Peace and War.* New York: Harper & Bros., 1948.

Trefousse, Hans L.   *Germany and American Neutrality, 1939-1941.* New York: Bookman Associates, 1951.

Tugwell, Rexford G.   *The Democratic Roosevelt.* Garden City, N.Y.: Doubleday & Co., 1957.

Tully, Grace.   *F.D.R. My Boss.* New York: Charles Scribner's Sons, 1949.

U.S. Department of State.   *Peace and War: United States Foreign Policy, 1931-1941.* Washington, D.C.: Government Printing Office, 1943.

U.S. Department of War.   *United States Army in World War II. Chief of Staff: Prewar Plans and Preparations,* by Mark Skinner Watson. Washington, D.C.: Government Printing Office, 1950.

Warburg, James P.   *The Long Road Home: The Autobiography of a Maverick.*

Garden City, N.Y.: Doubleday & Co., 1964.
Welles, Sumner. *The Time for Decision.* New York and London: Harper & Bros., 1944.
Wheeler-Bennett, John W. *King George VI: His Life and Reign.* New York: St. Martin's Press, 1958.
Williams, William Appleman. *The Tragedy of American Diplomacy.* New York: Dell Publishing Co., 1962
Wiltz, John E. *From Isolation to War, 1931-1941.* New York; Thomas Y. Crowell Co., 1968.

ARTICLES AND PERIODICALS

Billington, Ray Allen. "The Origins of Middle Western Isolationism." *Political Science Quarterly,* LX (March 1945) 44-46.
Borg, Dorothy. "Notes on Roosevelt's 'Quarantine' Speech." *Political Science Quarterly,* LXXII (September 1957), 405-33.
Cantril, Hadley. "America Faces the War: A Study in Public Opinion." *Public Opinion Quarterly,* IV (September 1940), 387-407.
————.; Donald Rugg; and Frederick Williams. "America Faces the War: Shifts in Opinion." *Public Opinion Quarterly*, IV (December 1940), 651-56.
Chicago Tribune. September 4, 1940.
Cole, Wayne S. "American Entry into World War II: A Historiographical Appraisal." *Mississippi Valley Historical Review,* XLIII (March 1957), 595-617.
Commager, Henry Steele. "America's Faith in Democracy." Review of *The Public Papers and Addresses of Franklin D. Roosevelt,* vols. VI-IX. *New York Times,* December 21, 1941, sec. 6, pp. 1, 7, 15.
Donovan, John C. "Congressional Isolationists and the Roosevelt Foreign Policy." *World Politics,* III (April 1951), 299-316.
"Gallup and Fortune Polls." *Public Opinion Quarterly*, V (March 1941), 133-65.
————. *Public Opinion Quarterly,* V (Fall 1941), 470-97.
————. *Public Opinion Quarterly,* VI (Spring 1942), 140-53.
Gleeck, L.E. "96 Congressmen Make Up Their Minds." *Public Opinion Quarterly,* IV (March 1940), 3-24.
Ickes, Harold L. "My Twelve Years With F.D.R." *Saturday Evening Post,* June 5, 1948, pp. 15-17, 78-92.
Jacob, Philip E. "Influence of World Events on U.S. 'Neutrality' Opinion." *Public Opinion Quarterly,* IV (March 1940), 48-65.
Lubell, Samuel. "Post-Mortem: Who Elected Roosevelt?" *Saturday Evening Post,* January 25, 1941, pp. 9-11, 91-96.
————. "Who Votes Isolationist and Why." *Harper's Magazine,* April 1951, pp. 29-36.
New York Times. June 27, 1940; September 4, 1940.
Nichols, Jeannette. "The Middle West and the Coming of World War II." *Ohio State Archaeological and Historical Quarterly,* LXII (1953), 122-45.

St. Louis Post-Dispatch.   "Inside Story of 'Propaganda Engine' to Send United States Army and Navy Equipment to Britain," by Charles G. Ross, September 22, 1940.

Roosevelt, Franklin D.   "Shall We Trust Japan?" *Asia*, XXIII (July 1923), 475-78, 526-29.

Schlesinger, Arthur M., Jr.   "As the world moved toward war, FDR watched and worked for peace." Review of *Franklin D. Roosevelt and Foreign Affairs*, vols. I-III, by Edgar B. Nixon (ed.). *New York Times,* July 6, 1969, sec. 7, pp. 1-2, 20-21.

Smuckler, Ralph H.   "The Region of Isolationism." *American Political Science Review*, XLVII (June 1953), 386-401.

Twohey, James S.   "An Analysis of Newspaper Opinion on War Issues." *Public Opinion Quarterly*, V (Fall 1941), 448-55.

Weinberg, Gerhard L. "Hitler's Image of the United States," *American Historical Review*, LXIX (July 1964), 1006-21

UNPUBLISHED MATERIALS

Fleron, Frederic J   "The Isolationists and the Foreign Policy of F.D.R.: A Study in Executive Leadership." Unpublished master's thesis, Brown University, 1961.

Radway, Laurence I.   "Administrative History of the Advisory Commission to the Council of National Defense, May 1940 to December 1940." U.S. Bureau of the Budget, unpublished manuscript, National Archives.

Tauber, Adele S.   "The Aid 'We' Rendered: Germany and the American Political Conventions of 1940." Unpublished master's thesis, Tufts University, 1968.

INDEX